MacCARTHY ON IMPEACHMENT

How to Find and Use These Weapons of Mass Destruction

TERENCE F. MacCARTHY
SEAN P. MacCARTHY
HONORABLE TERENCE F. MacCARTHY

Cover design by ABA Design.

Printed in the United States of America.

ISBN 978-1-63425-420-5

Discounts are available for books ordered in bulk. Special consideration is given to state bars, CLE programs, and other bar-related organizations. Inquire at Book Publishing, ABA Publishing, American Bar Association, 321 N. Clark Street, Chicago, Illinois 60654-7598.

www.ShopABA.org

DEDICATION

With great pleasure I dedicate this book to three outstanding women, all of whom have had a positive influence on my life.

Marian MacCarthy: My wonderful and dedicated wife for over fifty-four years. She has been and is the most important person in my life.

Carol Brook: Professionally, she has been the most wonderful person in my life. In the best decision I made as the Federal Defender, I hired Carol out of law school in 1976. Much success in our office was her doing. She, for the last seven years, has improved the office.

Dean Deryl Dantzler: The recently retired Dean of the National Criminal Defense College is both a friend and someone special. Her contributions to the teaching of trial advocacy have been significant. In a word, she is responsible for as good a trial advocacy program I have taught at – and I have taught at many.

Terence F. MacCarthy

With gratitude, I dedicate this book to my coauthors who have represented indigent criminal defendants a combined 70 years.

Sean P. MacCarthy

I humbly dedicate this book to the lawyers who toil in courtrooms, and in particular, the lawyers who represent marginalized people in society. And of course, I dedicate it to four wonderful, talented, and unique children: Jude, Catherine, Terence, and Patrick.

The Honorable Terence F. MacCarthy

ABOUT THE AUTHORS

Terence F. MacCarthy is the Defender Emeritus of the Federal Defender Program in the United States District Court for the Northern District of Illinois. For forty-two years he served as the Executive Director of the Chicago office. He also served as an Illinois Special Assistant Attorney General, specializing in civil trials and appeals. His criminal experience is primarily in the federal courts where he has tried and appealed many cases, and worked with his staff attorneys in preparing and trying additional cases. MacCarthy is one of the nation's most sought-after speakers at continuing legal education programs, having lectured in all 50 states and over a dozen foreign countries. He is the author of the American Bar Association top seller, *MacCarthy on Cross-Examination.*

Sean P. MacCarthy is a Partner with Chittenden, Murday & Novotny, LLC, a Chicago law firm. Sean graduated from the University of Illinois Champaign–Urbana in 1985, earning Phi Beta Kappa distinction. Sean received his J.D. degree in 1988 from Loyola University Chicago School of Law. Sean has tried cases in state courts and federal courts involving many areas including complex commercial matters, medical malpractice, and divorce. Sean also maintains an active pro-bono practice.

The Honorable Terence F. MacCarthy teaches Trial Advocacy extensively around the country to experienced lawyers as well as law students. As a faculty member for many distinguished Trial Advocacy programs he uses lectures, small group teaching, and improv to develop storytelling, communication, and advocacy skills. Terence served for twenty years with the Law Office of the Cook County Public Defender, working as both an Assistant Public Defender, and for his last seven years, as an Attorney Supervisor in the Felony Trial Division at the George N. Leighton Criminal Court Building at "26th and California." Terence was elected Judge of the Circuit Court of Cook County, Illinois, in 2010.

IMPEACHMENT
(Chapters)

Expert Witnesses

Extra

FOREWORD
Justice John Paul Stevens (Ret.)

Terry MacCarthy has been the Executive Director of the Federal Defender Program in the U.S. District Court for the Northern District of Illinois for a few years longer than I have been a member of the federal judiciary. He started his professional career as a law clerk to one of my favorite federal judges, William J. Campbell, the respected Chief Judge of the District Court for the Northern District of Illinois.

Terry's reputation as a public defender is unexcelled. A few years ago his book about cross-examination was published by the American Bar Association and has been well received by the profession.

In this new work—*MacCarthy on Impeachment*—jointly authored with his two sons, Terry has produced an equally valuable study of a subject even more specialized than the art of cross-examination. The book is subtitled *How to Find and Use These Weapons of Mass Destruction*. It separately identifies sixteen different ways to impeach a witness and includes fascinating examples of each, sprinkled with advice about how to maximize the impact on the jury and pitfalls to be avoided. Trial lawyers will no doubt be the principal beneficiaries of the book, but other readers will also enjoy Terry's breezy style and his selection of illustrative dialogues between defense counsel and hypothetical witnesses. This work is a welcome addition to the literature on a critical aspect of trial practice.

INTRODUCTION

Impeachment means one thing to nonlawyers and something totally different to trial lawyers. Most people, understandably, think of impeachment as proceedings to remove someone who serves in a high office. To trial lawyers it means something quite different. Obviously, as trial lawyers, we are interested in impeaching adverse witnesses. Though we are not seeking to remove them from office, we are seeking to discredit and make them look bad.

"Counsel you may cross-examine." These frequently heard terms are an invitation to cross-examine the witness from the trial judge. Though the first option is not mentioned, the next two are spelled out in Federal Rule of Evidence 611(b).[1]

The first option, one that precludes doing either of the other two options, is that the trial lawyer may waive her right to cross-examine. There are times when exercising this option is appropriate, though in truth and in fact, this option is an exception not often used.

Interestingly, when exercised, this first option of waiving cross-examination is usually done in an unnecessary, improper, and gratuitous manner. "This witness said nothing important so I have no need to cross-examine him." Or "What the witness told us has nothing to do with this case." Or simply "Cross-examination would be an unnecessary waste of time." Trial judges, showing amazing patience, seldom if ever correct the lawyer. The argument might be made that in exchange for shortening the trial the trial judge indulges the lawyer's slight misstep.

---

[1]Fed. R. Evid. 611(b). "Scope of Cross-Examination. Cross-Examination should not go beyond the subject matter of the direct examination and matters affecting the witness's credibility. The court may allow inquiry into additional matters as if on direct examination."

Assuming the cross-examination is not waived, which it seldom will be, you as the cross-examiner have two remaining options, the two spelled out in FRE 611(b). In all probability you will use both.

The second option allows you to cross-examine on "the subject matter of the direct examination." You may wish to use cross-examination to clarify, change, or challenge what the witness said on direct examination. For that matter, contrary to the teaching of some cross-examiners, you may repeat some of the direct, assuming of course, that something said on direct examination is helpful to your case.

Trial judges, most properly, interpret "the subject matter of direct" most liberally.

The third option is what this book is all about. We are told we may cross-examine on "matters affecting the credibility of the witness." Usually, most of our cross-examination will be directed to option two, the subject matter of the direct – in other words, what the witness said. Still, where available, we will delightfully use option three, which is referred to, if not with total accuracy, as concerning "matters affecting credibility."

We do not believe that we have ever heard a trial lawyer or a trial judge refer to crossing "on matters affecting credibility." We have a much better and more accurate and appropriate term we use.

We impeach.

We are not unmindful that "matters affecting credibility" is often referred to as "that which challenges veracity." Again, this is not a totally accurate definition of what we do when we impeach a witness. Yes, impeachment may go to the credibility and veracity of the witness, and usually it does. But impeachment can and sometimes does go beyond credibility and veracity.

Sure, impeachment is usually intended to show the witness is a liar, or at least mistaken.[2] But, contrary to the "credibility" or "veracity" language,

[2]Interestingly, we usually ask trial lawyers which they would prefer to prove, that the witness is a liar or simply mistaken. Most give the wrong answer. Most say they would prefer to prove the witness to be a liar. Actually, showing the witness to simply be mistaken is easier to do and is an easier and better sell to a jury. Then again, frequently you do not get to make this choice. You must go for the jugular and prove the witness to be a liar.

proper impeachment may fall short of "liar" or "mistaken." You may simply want to show that the witness "has a dog in the fight." Though you cannot prove the witness is a "liar" or "mistaken," you can prove that he has a motive or reason to favor one party or dislike the other party. This would be motivation impeachment. Ok, maybe this is close enough to "credibility" and "veracity." So let us go to something that has no relationship to "credibility" or "veracity."

Might you, as a cross-examiner, want to show that the witness is simply a "bad person," albeit a "bad person" who is credible? Of course you would. Interestingly, in New York this is permitted, and indeed encouraged.

What about the other states and the federal courts? With its common law origins, we have FRE 609. This rule, or some variation of the rule, has been for the most part adopted throughout the country. (Obviously a few states have adopted evidence rules which differ from the Federal Rules of Evidence. We mention a few of these, but we encourage you to review applicable state rules). Rule 609 allows us, under certain circumstances, to impeach a witness with a conviction. The conviction may not have involved a crime relating to "credibility" or "veracity." The chances are just as good that credibility or veracity were not involved in the conviction. For instance, take the murderer who pleads guilty and is therefore convicted. From the beginning our murderer confessed to what he had done. What we have is a credible murderer who has a conviction. That conviction, under appropriate circumstances, which has nothing to do with "credibility" or "veracity," can be used to impeach him should he appear as a witness.

So, also, when we use a learned treatise, FRE 803(18) (see Chapter 17), to impeach an expert, "credibility" or "veracity" is probably not an issue.

Actually, this point will be further and better developed when we talk about the potential for "bonus point" impeachment. Once you have properly entered the door of certain areas of impeachment, you may well be entitled to claim "bonus points," which usually will not relate to "credibility" or "veracity."

In sum, trial lawyers and trial judges call what we do impeachment, and it may have nothing to do with credibility or veracity.

Impeachment – A Confusing and Difficult Thing to Understand and to Do

Yes, impeachment is an alien, mystifying, and obtrusive area of the law. For the trial lawyer and judge, this is one of the most confusing and misunderstood parts of the trial, for several reasons.

First off, the law of impeachment is for the most part to be found in the law of evidence, unfortunately, though impeachment involves different applications of the law of evidence.

Second, the "state of the art"[3] leaves much to be desired. Though there are many excellent books on both evidence and trial advocacy, none of them do an adequate job of instructing the trial lawyer, or for that matter the trial and even appellate judges, on what they should and must know about the law of impeachment.[4]

Third, and finally, once acquainted with the law of impeachment the trial lawyer must be taught "how" to most effectively actually impeach a witness.

This comment always reminds us of a trial advocacy story told by Mike Wims, a Utah prosecutor, who spent many years trying Uniform Code of Military Justice cases as an extremely competent Air Force JAG officer. His opponent was cross-examining one of Mike's witnesses. The witness said something that the cross-examining attorney disagreed with. Suddenly, the lawyer simply told the witness that he was "impeached!" Possibly the right idea, but absolutely the wrong way to go about it.

Over the past few years, when lecturing on impeachment, we have asked how many trial lawyers had ever heard a talk on impeachment. The surprising response was less than five percent.

As a result of this history of confusion and neglect, the understanding of impeachment leaves much to be desired. Many, if not most, trial lawyers do not know what they *cannot* do in impeaching. They do not know what they *can* do. Most importantly, they do not know *how to do* what they can do.

Just as cross-examination is the most difficult of trial skills, impeachment, usually a part of cross-examination, is the most difficult of the difficult.

---

[3]Actually, impeachment does not involve an "art," but rather involves a science.

[4]Most of these books tell us there are five ways to impeach a witness. As you will see, there are no less than sixteen ways to impeach a witness.

Impeachment offers trial lawyers "weapons of mass destruction." We will now not only find those "weapons of mass destruction," but also learn about them and how to use them.

How This Book Came about

For many years senior MacCarthy lectured on "Impeachment with Inconsistent Statements." Several years ago the Florida Public Defenders asked him to do his talk on impeachment. They told him he would have five hours to cover the subject. He explained that his "Impeachment with Inconsistent Statements" talk only took two hours. They suggested he expand his talk to cover all methods of impeachment. There was plenty of lead time, and the challenge sounded interesting. He agreed.

One evening the following week, with no interruptions from visits or phone calls, the challenging project started.

How to start the project was easy. A list of all the ways a trial lawyer might impeach a witness was necessary. Relying on his own unillustrious career as a trial lawyer, he anticipated that he had impeached witnesses over two dozen ways. Now, to list them.

An hour later his list reached to only seven ways to impeach – a far cry from the anticipated two dozen.

Actually each time a supposedly new way to impeach came to mind, upon analysis, the supposed new way was actually a mere variation of one of the original seven ways. For some time, we stayed stuck on seven.

One would think answers and suggestions would be available in the otherwise thorough and excellent books on trial advocacy or books on evidence. Such was not the case. For that matter, the books only mentioned ways already included or covered.

Notwithstanding extensive trial experience, we were surprised and disappointed at what little we knew about impeachment, and in particular the various ways to impeach a witness. Similarly, we were disappointed that there was nothing extant to assist us.

Eventually, the seven expanded to nine. This resulted in a moment of major trauma. In conversation, an excellent trial lawyer, indeed the senior litigator in a large and well-respected law firm which had invited senior MacCarthy to lecture on cross-examination, allowed that he knew where we got our list of nine ways to impeach. Obviously, this was impossible – they were the product of much original, if not exhaustive, thought. He then reminded us that Professor Irving Younger had, years before, given a talk on "The Nine Ways to Impeach a Witness."

This all but ended our project. Then again one of us, having been reminded, remembered Professor Younger's talk. As great a lecturer as the Professor was – one of the best ever – this was not one of his better presentations. Fortunately, the lawyer who mentioned the Professor Younger talk had a copy, which he would and did send to us.

It was opened anxiously when it arrived. The first of Professor Younger's nine ways to impeach convinced us that we were on the right track and should continue. Not only were his nine ways *not the same as our nine* ways, though obviously some were the same, but his first one was not even on our list. Professor Younger's first way was to impeach on the witnesses' oath. These past few years of giving talks on impeachment have allowed us to ask if anyone had ever impeached a witness on their oath. None had. Therefore, we would not, and have not, added it to our book.

We always wondered where Professor Younger came up with the idea of impeaching a witness on their oath. Senior MacCarthy, who in this dotage enjoys reading history and old cases, as obviously Professor Younger did, discovered a plausible explanation.

The famous, or if you prefer infamous trial of Queen Caroline in 1820 may, indeed probably does, provide the answer.

The Queen was defended by Lord Brougham, a brilliant man and most probably the leading barrister or trial lawyer of his day. Many of the witnesses against the Queen were Italian.

Brougham objected to the proprietary and sufficiency of Catholic Italians taking the oath of a witness. The panel of judges who served as advisers to the peers (the House of Lords) concluded the oath was satisfactory.

Brougham's objection went to competency to testify. Though he lost that argument he probably could have, but apparently did not, impeach the witnesses making the same point.

The other of Professor Younger's nine ways, though several were similar to the ones on our list, were not covered particularly well.

A short time later the nine ways were no longer of importance. We got our list up to thirteen ways to impeach, and finally up to the present sixteen ways. Yes, there may even be more!

Say whatever, at least Professor Younger listed nine ways to impeach a witness. Most trial advocacy books usually list only five ways to impeach a witness. Indeed, the National Judicial College materials used to teach judges, instruct that there are but five methods of impeachment. No wonder both judges and trial lawyers have problems understanding the subject of impeachment.

The Sixteen Ways to Impeach

You will now have a list of the sixteen ways to impeach a witness. It should serve you well as you prepare for trial.

Importantly, you will not only have the list of the "sixteen" ways to impeach, but the list appears in a designated order. The "sixteen" ways are listed *in order of importance.*

What makes one method of impeachment more important than another? Three things: (1) *How often* will you get to use it; (2) What is its *impact* with the jury when you use it; and (3) Are there *evidentiary limitations* when you use it. Obviously, the first and second factors improve the position of the impeachment method. The third consideration works to lower the position of the impeachment method.

The list uses three lines, all intended to be of some importance. The top two lines suggest a substantial and significant difference between impeachment methods one and two, and then again between methods eight and nine.

The line over impeachment method fifteen is intended to tell us that the last two methods, fifteen and sixteen, are not in order of importance. Rather, the line tells us that these methods apply only to expert witnesses.

Summarizing the list we know that the first method, inconsistent statement impeachment, is by and away the most important of the methods of impeachment by a long shot.

Methods two through eight are important. Conversely, methods nine through fourteen are the least important ways to impeach. Finally, as earlier mentioned, methods fifteen *and* sixteen are not intended to be listed in order of importance, but rather are limited to expert witnesses.

WAYS TO IMPEACH

[1] Inconsistent Statements (FRE 613)

[2] Contradictions – Contrary Evidence

[3] Motivation

[4] Truthfulness (FRE 608)

[5] Convictions (FRE 609)

[6] What the Witness Could Have Done but Did Not Do

[7] Capacity

[8] Bad Acts, Crimes, and Wrongs (FRE 404(b))

[9] Habit (FRE 406)

[10] Writing Used to Refresh Memory (FRE 612)

[11] Admissions (FRE 801(d)(2))

[12] The Hearsay Declarant (FRE 806)

[13] Character Witnesses

[14] Certain Evidence of Sexual Behavior by the Alleged Victim of the Defendant (FRE 412, 413, 414, 415)

Experts Only

[15] Qualifications and Curriculum Vitae (FRE 702)

[16] Learned Treatises (FRE 803(18))

CHAPTER 1

Impeachment with Inconsistent Statements

This is the most important of the methods of impeachment. If for no other reason, it is the most important because it is the impeachment method most used by trial lawyers. When you stop and think about it you will agree that somewhere in the neighborhood of seventy percent of the time you impeach a witness, it will be with an inconsistent statement.

It has a good, if not outstanding, "impact" score. It does not carry the "impact" of a FRE 609 impeachment with a conviction. Still, you are scoring points by showing the witness is either a liar or at the least mistaken.[1]

There are legal limitations on inconsistent statement impeachment. The first, spelled out in FRE 613(b), should not create a problem if you follow the "Fishing Rules"[2] in perfecting your impeachment. (See specifically Fishing Rule #4.) FRE 613(b) requires you to allow the witness an opportunity to explain or deny the statement, which seems to suggest you show the witness the statement. We thought we did away with the Rule in Queen

---

[1]As mentioned, most would opt for "liar." Indeed, particularly in criminal cases, this may be the only alternative available. That said, however, when given your choice opt for "mistaken," this is a much easier sell to the jury.

[2]We use and teach the "Six Fishing Rules" to suggest how to impeach with an inconsistent statement. This will be explained later.

Caroline's Case.[3] (Again, see Fishing Rule #4.) This should not present a problem. Out Fishing Rule #4 requires you show the witness the statement.

The second limitation is not spelled out in FRE 613, but it does apply. Inconsistent statement impeachment is subject to the "collateral" limitation. If the inconsistent statement is "collateral," or if you will, not particularly important (this will be further explained in the presentation of Fishing Rule #2), you will not be able to prove the inconsistent statement through "extrinsic evidence."[4]

How important is impeachment with an inconsistent statement? Put it this way – it is as if (no, this will not happen) you were to start by addressing the jury and representing to them that you are about to prove that the witness is either a liar or totally mistaken. Obviously, you better deliver.

In truth and in practice, most trial lawyers are neither comfortable nor skilled when it comes to impeaching with an inconsistent statement.

Confronted with the witness who suddenly insists the car was red and not green, as mentioned in what will be the inconsistent statement, less experienced lawyers want to gently strike their forehead, curse to themselves, and reluctantly proceed to do a seven-second impeachment. It goes something like this: "You said something else to someone else sometime else." Obviously, this does not do justice to the potential of impeachment.

Conversely, an experienced trial lawyer, when presented with the same situation will rejoice. They do not hit themselves in the forehead. Rather than curse to themselves, they look to heaven and give thanks to their God.

They give thanks that their God has just done them an enormous favor. Their case is weak, and up until then they had little, if anything, to work with. Now their God has given them this great gift.

They proceed with alacrity and not reluctance. For that matter, their impeachment will take more than seven seconds. How long will it take? This usually depends upon just how bad their case is. The worse the case, the longer the impeachment will be. This may be the only time during the trial when they are "looking good" and scoring points. This is the type of impeachment we will strive to emulate.

---

[3]*The Queen's Case*, 2 Br. & B. 284, 129 Eng. Rep. 976 (1820).

[4]See the chapter on Truthfulness Impeachment, which is always "collateral." You will be provided possible ways to negate or offset the limitations of this rule of evidence.

The Law

To find out more about this subject you would look to the trial advocacy or evidence books, most probably under the heading Impeachment with Prior Inconsistent Statements. Truth be known, you will not find a great deal of particularly helpful information. Again, impeachment in general is not a popular subject.

Let us take those four terms, Impeachment with Prior Inconsistent Statement, and use them to talk about the law related to this subject.

IMPEACHMENT

Three issues are obvious. For the most part, only the third or last of these is of major importance to us as trial lawyers.

1. You may impeach your own witness (FRE 607)

Many think this rule was a great breakthrough – that it created something that was not there. This is not totally accurate.

At common law one could impeach their own witness. To do so you were required to show the judge you were "surprised" by what the witness had said. Trial lawyers, usually gifted in dramatics, found this requirement relatively easy. It required far less than falling to the floor in disgust or explaining: "Oh my God, how can you say that?" In any event, once the trial judge was satisfied that you were surprised by the answer of the witness, you could impeach your own witness.

This said, do you really want to impeach your own witness?

You may prefer to merely refresh recollection. (This is explained later.) Or you may wish to utilize a technique most experienced prosecutors have developed into an art form.

Prosecutor Direct: "What did you see?"
Witness: "A red car."
Prosecutor: "Was not the car you saw green?"
Defense Attorney: "Objection your Honor. The prosecutor is leading the witness."

Judge: "Sustained."
Prosecutor: "Now, once again, what color was the car you saw?"
Witness: "Come to think of it, it was green and not red."

Impeaching your own witness is not something experienced trial lawyers are anxious to do. This is particularly so when it comes to criminal defense lawyers.

This said, we read with much interest, and even more skepticism, the suggestion of former Chief Justice Warren Burger that criminal defense lawyers impeach their defendants when they believe the witness is perjuring himself.[5] Carrying this suggestion out to its natural conclusion creates, at best, a comical and ridiculous scenario.

In any event, FRE 607 is not all that much a new thing. For that matter, many judges still require the showing of "surprise" before allowing the impeachment. Also, there is understandable judicial concern when a lawyer puts a witness on the stand with the purpose of getting in impeaching material.[6]

2. Some inconsistent statement impeachment comes in as "substantive evidence"

This again appears to be a major change and a major consideration. Although this is a major change, most trial lawyers, with the obvious exception of federal prosecutors, are not concerned with or affected by it.

At common law the inconsistent statement used to impeach came in only to impeach the witness. It did not come in as "substantive evidence." For most trial lawyers this posed no problems. Trial lawyers were more than satisfied to have the jury hear the impeaching statement. At the very least it raised serious questions, usually about the truthfulness, and,

[5] *Nix v. Whiteside,* 475 U.S. 157, 169 (1986).
[6] *See McCormick on Evidence* § 38 at 141 n.10 (Rosenstiel et al. eds., 5th ed. 1999) (Surprise is required by several statutes, D.C. Code § 14-104; Ga. Code § 38-1801 (if "entrapped"); and Ohio R. Evid. 607. The concept of "surprise" varies in the various jurisdictions. Sometimes "actual" or genuine surprise is required; in other decisions it is not. *See* Comment, 49 Va.L.Rev. 996 (1963)).

at the very least, the accuracy of the witness's testimony. Also, when the impeachment was properly done (as described in the Fishing Rules), the jury believed the truth and accuracy of the impeaching statement and not the witness's testimony. The traditional cautionary instruction, that the impeaching statement could be considered only to impeach, as with most cautionary instructions, had little effect on the jury's thinking. Once they have seen the pink elephant it does little good to tell them they did not see the pink elephant. As Justice Jackson said, "[t]he naive assumption that prejudicial effects can be overcome by instructions to the jury. . . all practicing lawyers know to be unmitigated fiction."[7]

Our favorite explanation of this issue is to be found in the wonderful movie *Anatomy of a Murder*. During his cross-examination of a doctor, criminal defense attorney Jimmy Stewart asks a question the judge rules to be improper. The witness answered the question before the judge could rule on the objection. The judge then gives the jury the traditional "curative instruction" to disregard both the question and the answer.

This was the end of the cross-examination and Stewart returned to counsel table where the defendant whispered to him "how can the jury disregard what they just heard"? Stewart's short but accurate reply, which he repeated twice was, "They can't."

What then was the problem, and why the change?

One group of trial lawyers, few in number but incredibly persuasive, had a problem with the common law limitation on how the impeaching statement was treated. We refer to federal prosecutors. Truth be known, their concerns before FRE 801(d)(1) were real.

To explain. In a major investigation into mob activities, it would not be uncommon for federal agents and prosecutors to put pressure on "Mr. Small." The pressure would usually come in the way of threats, and occasionally promises. Either you cooperate with us or terrible things will happen to you. On the other hand, of course, if you cooperate, the terrible things would not occur, and for that matter good things will come your way.

Not surprisingly, "Mr. Small" often got the message. The cooperation required was to give evidence against "Mr. Big." To make the threats go

---

[7]*Krulewitch v. United States*, 336 U.S. 440, 453 (1949) (Jackson, J., concurring).

away and earn the goodies offered, "Mr. Small" would indeed give information against "Mr. Big."

The next step required "Mr. Small" to appear and testify before a federal grand jury. When this was done "Mr. Big" was indicted and eventually tried.

However, as often was the case, still another group of individuals, friends of "Mr. Big," also approached "Mr. Small" before the trial. Once again, there were threats and warnings. In the words of the trade, "Mr. Big's" friend made "offers he could not refuse."

"Mr. Small," obviously not to be envied, was between a "rock and a hard place." However, nature being what it is, "Mr. Small" understandably considered the "offer he could not refuse" to be the more substantial of the threats. He decided to change his mind and to renege on his agreement with the prosecutors.

Now the moment of truth – actually, a poor play on words. "Mr. Small" is called to the stand by the federal prosecutors. Unsuspiciously, or maybe not so, the federal prosecutor asks him what he knows about the defendant, "Mr. Big." "Mr. Who?" "I never heard of him."

Recall we earlier talked about the right to impeach your own witness, even before the Federal Rules of Evidence. An experienced prosecutor could and would easily show the required "surprise," be it real or simply necessary.

Using the grand jury testimony, "Mr. Small" could and would be effectively impeached. Moreover, as already mentioned, the jury was inclined to believe the truth of the grand jury testimony. Still, the prosecutor had a problem.

The grand jury testimony came in "merely to impeach." It did not come in as substantive evidence.

If, as often was the circumstance, "Mr. Small's" grand jury testimony was the only evidence against "Mr. Big," the prosecutor would lose the case when "Mr. Big's" defense attorney made a motion for judgment of acquittal at the close of the prosecution's case-in-chief.

Given the chance, would the jury have convicted, cautionary instruction notwithstanding? Of course. The jury would accept and believe what he told the grand jury, rather than his new version or story told on the stand. But without substantive evidence the judge was required to grant the motion for judgment of acquittal.

So you see, federal prosecutors did have a real problem. They wanted the impeachment with inconsistent statement to come in not merely to impeach, but as substantive evidence.

In major part they got what they wanted. The result, FRE 801(d)(1), allows an inconsistent statement to come in as substantive evidence if the impeaching statement was given under oath.

Obviously, as intended, this takes care of the federal prosecutors when they use grand jury statements.

Many trial attorneys and evidence teachers misread the requirement by mistakenly adding a second requirement, that the inconsistent statement was also subject to cross-examination. This is not so for if it were, grand jury statements, the intended purpose of the rule change, would not come in as substantive evidence. The "subject to cross-examination" requirement does not apply to the impeaching statement, but rather the witnesses' appearance at trial.

For additional information, if not further elucidations, you may read *California v. Green*, 399 U.S. 149 (1970), which preceded FRE 801(d)(1).

So where does all of this leave trial lawyers who are not federal prosecutors? For the most part, you are back to where you started and where you are content to be. The jury, under all circumstances, gets to hear the inconsistent statement when you impeach the witness with it.

The only change would occur where the inconsistent statement was under oath, most probably during a deposition. Given this situation, you should request the judge instruct the jury that "the impeaching statement comes in not merely to impeach the witness but as substantive evidence as well."

Wait a minute; you appear to be talking out of both sides of your mouth – not unlike the witness. Earlier you said that as long as the inconsistent impeachment comes in and the jury hears it, it is not important to trial lawyers, other than federal prosecutors, that it comes in as substantive evidence. Yes, this is what we said and we stand by it. However, the opportunity to have the trial judge call attention to the impeaching statement and in effect "loop" it would help and not hurt. Besides, if you are a criminal defense lawyer and the judge denies your request for the instruction, you will have still another "harmless error" argument for the appellate court.

3. The collateral/noncollateral issue

When you impeach with an inconsistent statement, you will be subject to the *collateral–noncollateral* limitation. In other words, sometimes your impeachment will be *collateral.* This means you will be limited to accepting the witness's answer, even though you have the witness's statement that would, in effect, show him to be at least mistaken or, more probably, a double liar. The law of evidence declares that where the impeachment is collateral, the witness statement is not material to the case, and may therefore not be introduced. This rule is intended to save trial time, which, to a point, is understandable. But our supposed quest for "truth" pays a substantial price to maintain this rule of evidence and to speed up the trial.

In any event, this is a limitation on your right to properly impeach with an inconsistent statement.

So the question we should now ask is how do we, as trial lawyers and trial judges, know whether what is being used to impeach is "collateral"? Or, is it not subject to this evidentiary limitation in that it is "noncollateral"?

This is an important question and one that must and will be answered. But not yet. There will be a far more propitious time to explain this issue when we cover "how to impeach with an inconsistent statement." More specifically, the "collateral–noncollateral" rule of evidence will be explained in the context of actual impeachment (the best way to teach and understand the law of evidence) when we cover Fishing Rule 2, Setting the Hook, or, as it is usually called by others, "recommitting" the witness.

PRIOR

Lawyers and, in particular, evidence teachers, love this term, "prior." Obviously we, as trial lawyers, should not like this term. Still, you will usually find inconsistent statement impeachment referred to with the conditioning term "prior."

We strongly suggest simply eliminating the term "prior." We suggest it be eliminated for three reasons.

1. The use of the term "prior" violates our Trial Advocacy Rule 11.[8] Rule 11 tells us we should speak in a courtroom as we would speak in a bar. "I would like the same drink I had prior." Obviously, we have in mind a nice bar, necessarily one with carpeting on the floor.

What a wonderful rule. Does or should this rule give us a tax reason or excuse to visit bars so we can practice learning how to speak as a trial lawyer?

"What did you do *prior* to coming to this bar?" Obviously, this does not pass the Rule 11 litmus test. The point is then made that if it is not appropriate for use in the bar, it is not appropriate for our use as trial lawyers.

As an aside, we and many other trial lawyers appreciate and follow the teachings of Rule 11. In a word, the rule commends to us the suggestion that we spend some time in bars so we can practice speaking as trial lawyers.

2. "Prior" is a redundant term, and therefore a totally unnecessary one.

Think as you may, you cannot come up with a single example of an inconsistent statement that will be used to impeach that was not made "before" the start of impeachment. All statements used to impeach of necessity were made "prior" or before the impeachment.

3. This reason is not as obvious unless, of course, you are familiar with our slavish dedication to trilogies. In a word, you should strive to always have three points – as we learned from the ancient Greeks; this improves your communication or rhetoric.

This said, the third reason to eliminate the term "prior" becomes more obvious. Once eliminated, we are left with three terms: "*Impeachment*," "*Inconsistent*," and "*Statements*." This is where we want to be.

---

[8]MacCarthy's Rules of Trial Advocacy are included at the end of this book.

INCONSISTENT

In obedience to our suggestion[9] that you use trilogies, it naturally follows that there are three things that are "inconsistent" when it comes to impeaching a witness statement.

1. Contrary

This, the most obvious and indeed the most used reason to impeach, is a contrary response by the witness. The witness testimony, be it on direct or on cross, is "contrary" to what is included in a statement made by the witness.

On direct or cross-examination, the witness tells us the car was red. In his statement to be used to impeach, the witness said the car was *green*. Red and green are contrary, and you may impeach.

Contrary statements need not be diametrically opposed. It can include a change in position where the truth of one statement implies falsity of the other statement, and thus, the two statements are irreconcilably at odds.

2. Omissions

If the witness's impeaching statement does not mention something the witness now states when testifying – and that *something* is *important* – you may impeach on the omission.

An example, one involving criminal law, would be appropriate.

Late one evening, patrolling in a dangerous area, a police officer sees (actually, they never see something, they "observe") a car. The police stop the car. The officer with the largest shoe size kicks out one of the rear lights. A defective rear light gives probable cause for the stop. In the stopped car are four men, the driver and one passenger in the front and two in the backseat. The car is registered in the name of a woman, the girlfriend of the driver.

The officers see ("observe") a plastic bag in the backseat. Checking its contents, they correctly determine it is a bag of marijuana. The driver is indicted.

Two days before the trial, the able but overworked prosecutor finally gets to interview the arresting police officer.

---

[9] *See* Rule 3 of MacCarthy's Rules of Trial Advocacy.

The prosecutor is less than pleased with the interview. He explains to the arresting officer that they have no case. How do they prove the marijuana in the backseat belonged to the defendant driver? In the first place, it was not his car. The two people in the backseat were closer and had easier access to the bag than the driver. Simply stated, they cannot prove it was the driver's marijuana.

Realizing he was no longer a hero, but rather a dolt, the officer decides to reverse and correct the situation.

"You have a case. Just ask me what the driver said when I picked up the bag." The prosecutor responds: "I have your official police report in front of me and there is no mention of the driver saying anything except for giving you his name and the name of the owner of the car."

"I know," responds the officer, "but just ask me this question and we will have a good case."

"If I ask you that question, what will your reply be?" asks the prosecutor. "I will testify," responds the police officer, "the driver said 'hey, watch out, I don't want you to spill *my* marijuana.'"

If this case were to go to trial and the police officer testified to the driver's statement, the officer could be impeached by the *omission* of the defendant's supposed statement in his police report, because the statement is important and should have been included in the officer's report.

Is this usually a powerful method of impeachment? No, it makes sense to be allowed to impeach on an omission, but the impact of this type of impeachment at times may not be that powerful. Still, it is available.

Interestingly, *MacCarthy on Cross-Examination* teaches that a cross-examiner should not ask questions. It does however, allow for a few, very few, exceptions. Impeaching with an omission may present an exception and the opportunity, indeed the need, to ask the witness a question.

"Officer, would you please read from your official police report where it mentions Mr. Smith's making a statement about the bag?"

On the plus side, he cannot read the statement from the report. On the negative side, this question may allow him to give an excuse why the statement is not in the report.

3. I Do Not Know–Remember–Recall

Surprisingly, many trial lawyers do not know that these responses during cross-examination, "I do not know;" "I do not remember;" or "I do not recall," may be impeached as an inconsistent statement.

Going back to basic cross-examination, the better way to handle this would be to simply "tweak" the witness. You "tweak" the witness by simply repeating the original statement. However, as explained in *MacCarthy on Cross-Examination*, your opponent may object "asked and answered"; (the more appropriate objection should be "cumulative" and the trial judge might sustain the objection). Or, of course, even if there is no objection or the trial judge does not sustain a "asked and answered" objection, the witness may persist with the evasive nonresponsive answer.

In any event, a not-too-swift trial judge or a persistent witness may preclude your ability to successfully "tweak" the witness. Yes, you may then impeach the witness, though in practice you will probably not do so, at least not right away.

The evasive responses historically used eighty-seven times by the witness Majocchi[10] when being cross-examined by Lord Brougham in *Queen Caroline's* case, and later made famous by Kato Kalin in the *O.J. Simpson* case and then used extensively by former Attorney General Gonzales ("I cannot recall") can and usually should be handled short of impeachment. You have alternatives.

There are three ways to punish the witness or, as we prefer, the "puppy." The least invasive way is to simply "tweak" the puppy by repeating the statement. Moving up the food chain to more severe punishment you may, in response to the evasive nonanswer, hit the witness with a Joe Louis-style, short, six-inch punch. This, we trial lawyers know, is called "refreshing recollection." We know what it is called but, often, we are not sure how to do it.

Later we will do some Trial Advocacy 101 and explain how to show a witness a document. Now we will only cover the last step in showing a witness a document we wish to use to "refresh recollection."

Obviously, the document you will use is the one that has the witness's proper response to the statement you have just put to him.

[10] "No me recuerdo": "I don't remember."

"You know what this is?" Importantly, all you want is simply "yes." You do not want, and have no need for, the witness to explain what the document is.

"Read the highlighted portion to yourself, not out loud." You have highlighted the specific area you want read.

After the witness has read the highlighted portion, take back the document. Now simply renew your statement. Having just read the answer, indeed his answer, the witness should give you your "yes." You will have properly refreshed his recollection.

Should the witness persist in the evasive, nonresponsive answer after reading his earlier answer to the same question, then get out your Louisville Slugger bat and give the witness a good whack – in a word, impeach him with the statement.

STATEMENT

FRE 801(a) tells us what a statement is. It can appear in the form of something spoken by the witness. Also, it can appear in the form of a written assertion. Finally, it can appear as nonverbal conduct intended as an assertion.[11]

For impeachment purposes, the major issue is whose statement is it. To impeach, it must be the witness's statement. Obviously, something the witness said or something they wrote would be their statement.

Reading and signing a statement written by someone else would be a witness statement assuming, of course, the witness provided the information.

In a word, mostly anything a witness says or writes will be an impeachable statement. On the other hand, a summary of what the witness said prepared by another might not necessarily be the witness's statement. This may raise an issue with FBI 302 statements. The statements are written by the agents. A few judges may find these are not the witness's statement. So be it. You may use contradiction which will be even better.

---

[11] *Harris v. N.Y.*, 401 U.S. 222 (1971); *Michigan v. Harvey*, 499 U.S. 344 (1990); *U.S. v. Almeida*, 341 F.3d 1318 (11th Cir. 2003).

That said, some statements are much better than others when it comes to impeachment. The more trappings, the better. It would follow that grand jury testimony, testimony rendered under oath in a court setting, deposition testimony, and statements made to the police; all would be better statements to impeach with. You can do more with them.

Conversely, an oral statement made to the bartender in Clancy's Pub, though an impeccable statement, would be less effective in practice.

In criminal cases, we know that statements taken of a defendant in violation of the Fifth or Sixth Amendments are involuntary and cannot be used against the defendant unless the defendant testifies,[12] in which case the statements unconstitutionally obtained may be used to *impeach.*

How to Impeach with an Inconsistent Statement "The Fishing Rules"

To teach and better remember how to impeach with an inconsistent statement we use a fishing analogy or, as observed by some, a "fishy" story.

Picture yourself on a beautiful Wisconsin spring-fed lake in early August. Temperature wise it is a perfect day. This is not a large lake and, indeed, the boat you will use is accordingly a small one, totally open and about twelve feet long. So also the motor is small, what fishermen would call a trolling motor.

Obviously you will take with you your fishing gear, none of it all that sophisticated or fancy. Two friends will join you, and, most importantly, you will bring along a case of "mother's milk," Guinness Stout.

Your method of fishing will be relatively simple. You will find a nice spot on the lake, hopefully one that the fish also appreciate. You will cast your line and basically do little else – save, of course, talk to your friends and, most importantly, enjoy your Guinness. You are using a red-and-white bobber. It sits on the water, and if it goes down under the water, you will know you have a fish.

We are ready to start fishing. It is not only important but indeed necessary that we learn and follow the Six Fishing Rules.

---

[12] *Massiah v. U.S.*, 377 U.S. 201 (1964); *Miranda v. Arizona*, 384 U.S. 436 (1966).

FISHING RULES

①
LET SMALL FISH GO:
EXCEPTIONS:
1) Hungry
2) No Big Fish
3) Lots Of Small Fish

②
SET HOOK:
Not If Fact Is Important

③
REEL FISH IN:
- Take Your Time
- Build Up Statement*
- Prevent Escape

④
NET FISH
Do Show Fish The Document
- FRE: Rule 613
- *Queen Caroline's Case* 129 Enc. Rep. 976, 2 B & B286 (1820)

⑤
KILL FISH
Who Reads Statement?
What If Fish Will Not Let You Kill It?

⑥
DO NOT PLAY WITH FISH

- The Second Time Around
- Clean, Cook, And Serve Fish (During Closing Argument)

* Fresh in Mind; Truth, Details, Important Details, Accurate, Rely Upon, Understood, Important To You.

Fishing Rule 1
"Let the Small Fish Go"

This is a rule of common sense. If the fish is smaller or the same size as your bait, do not bring it in. Rather, just give your rod a flip and get the small fish off of your line. This is important in that you know and appreciate that to otherwise bring in the undersized fish, you would need two hands to reel it in. You would have to put your Guinness down to do this. We do not stop drinking our Guinness unless we have a decent-size fish. (Some say we should never stop drinking the Guinness – the hell with the fishing!)

Taking our fishing analogy into the courtroom, the small fish usually appear in the form of the persnickety witness. We have all been subjected to these people.

The witness's statement records her as saying she left the music reception "around 3 p.m." Your properly executed cross-examination goes as follows:

Q: "You left the music reception?"
A: "Yes."
Q: "Around three in the afternoon?"
A: "No counsel. I left at exactly 2:58 and 30 seconds. I remember I looked at my watch and it was exactly 2:58 and 30 seconds."

In fairness, you should be able to punish or at least laugh at a witness such as this. But, of course, you cannot, or more to the point you should not.

Can you impeach her with her inconsistent statement? Yes, of course you can. But this rule tells you not to do so unless, of course, something important happened a minute and one-half before 3:00 p.m.

Remember, witnesses such as this do not come across well to the jury. Accepting this, we refrain from impeaching on the inconsistent statement.

There is an exception to this rule. It is, however, an exception that should seldom be used.

While fishing you became hungry; you have caught no large fish, but the persnickety witness has provided you with many small fish. Out of desperation your patience may finally come to an end. You eventually make the decision to bring in the small fish.

Use this exception hesitantly if at all. Our experience is that we use the exception more to satisfy our own desires, a desire to punish the witness, than to advance our case. Again, this is an exception that seldom should be used.

There is still a witness who does not deserve to be "hit with a Louisville Slugger bat." The honest-but-mistaken witness. What had seen a green car suddenly, on direct or cross, becomes a red car.

Going to the attack against this witness would be bad form.

You might first use the usually effective though improper, when used on direct, prosecutor method by simply, albeit pleasantly, correcting the witness. "Actually the car was green and not red."

If this does not work, you could refresh recollection.

And finally, as a last resort you could use the short version of impeachment. Simply mention the earlier statement and the fact the witness then said the car was green.

Fishing Rule 2
"Set the Hook"

Have you ever had the fish get away before you can get it in the boat? This results when you do not properly "set the hook."

Q: "You saw a car?"
A: "Yes."
Q: "Green?"
A: "No, it was red."

The witness statement said the car was green. You proceed with your impeachment, which for the most part is explained in Rule 3. When you have the fish near the boat the fish realizes it will soon be a dead fish. It must do something, and it does.

A: "Well actually counsel, you are partially correct. The car actually was that new red green color."

You have lost your opportunity to perfect your impeachment, to kill the fish. You lost the fish because you failed to "set the hook." You still scored points, but not as many as you wanted and expected.

We state the rule as "set the hook." N.I.T.A. has long taught us to do this, but they call it "recommitting" the witness.

"Setting the hook" or "recommitting," whatever you want to call it, is simple to explain and to do.

A: "No, it was red."
Q: "You are telling the jury the car was definitely red?"
A: "Yes."
Q: "You are telling them that the car was absolutely not green?"

The hook is set. It would now be difficult for the fish to give you the "red–green" afterthought.

So far so good. We know why we set the hook and how to do it. Now the problems and some confusion set in.

You do not always "set the hook." To explain this exception to Rule 2 we must understand the difference between impeachment that is collateral and impeachment which is *noncollateral.*

Assuming the color of the car, be it red or green, is not important to the case – your Johnny drove neither a red nor a green car. Then the inconsistent statement impeachment would be "collateral." The matter is deemed "*not important.*" You are still allowed to impeach for the purpose of suggesting the witness has given a contrary statement. Unfortunately, in that your impeachment will be "collateral," there will be limitations on your right to perfect your impeachment.

The law of evidence, for reasons we find difficult to agree with, finds it more important that the trial should move faster than the truth should come out. In a word, our evidence rules would allow a witness to lie with impunity. Proving the lie, we are told, would take time and therefore should not be allowed.

If, then, the inconsistent statement impeachment is collateral ("not that important") and the witness denies making the impeaching statement, you may not perfect your impeachment by using the statement, which is referred to as "extrinsic evidence."

Q: "In your deposition, you told us the car was green?"
A: "No, I said, as I am now, that the car was red."

End of impeachment. The deposition, where the witness said the car was green, is "extrinsic evidence." It cannot be shown or referred to the witness who is allowed lie with impunity.

When presented with "collateral" impeachment you will nonetheless follow the fishing rules.

In our chapter on "truthfulness" impeachment we do have a few suggestions as to how to impeach with a "collateral" statement if you believe the witness may deny making the statement. This is included in the chapter on "truthfulness" impeachment because all "truthfulness" impeachment is "collateral."

Noncollateral

Obviously, it follows if the color of the car is important, then the impeachment is "noncollateral" and you may use "extrinsic" statements. Simply explained, if your Johnny drove a red car and you do not want him associated with the car, the color of the car will be important.

Now we have a big problem, a problem with Rule 2, a problem with the conventional thinking that we should always "recommit." In a word, we do not and should not always "set the hook" or "recommit" when the matter is *noncollateral*, or important. Understand what we are now suggesting is contrary to the conventional wisdom.

Let us go into the courtroom and see what this is all about and why we come down where we do on the issue.

Accepting the red–green car issue is important, our primary goal or objective is to have the jury believe the car was green and not red. This is what is most important. Do we help or hurt this objective by "setting the hook?"

Q: "You are telling the jury the car was definitely red?"
A: "Yes."
Q: "You are telling them that the car was absolutely not green?"

Yes, the hook is set. It would be difficult for the fish to change from red to green. Think about it, would you not want the witness to change from red to green?

From a trial advocacy and communication perspective, is this really what you want? Remember that which is of paramount importance to your case – helping the jury believe the car was green.

To start with, when you recommit you are "looping" (repeating) the damaging story to the jury – the car was red, not green. This is questionable trial advocacy where you want the jury to believe the car was green.

Accepting this, as we suggest, we would not "set the hook" where the issue is important. We would not "loop" the bad into the jury box.

But if the "hook is not set," would it not be possible for the fish to get away? Yes, it would, but we would gladly let it get away. To explain: The only way the fish could get away would be by realizing and seeking to avoid its problem – by changing its story during the impeachment, by changing the color of the car from red to green.

Yes, then we would graciously allow the fish to spit out the hook and avoid its execution. We want, above all else, the green car.

But even in avoiding execution, the fish will have suffered greatly with the hook in its mouth. Though not executed it will have been scarred and punished. The fish's duplicity will not be lost on the jury.

Most importantly, we will have accomplished our main and most important objective: the car will be green and not red.

Fishing Rule 3
Reel the Fish in Slowly and with Purpose

Two of the three authors are fishermen. The other one, truth be known, has neither interest nor experience with fishing.

As a nonfisherman, the reaction and response to the red-and-white bobber going down under the water would reflect his inexperience. He would, in his excitement, want the fish in the boat as soon as possible. To this end he would attempt to bring the fish in immediately. He is both big and strong enough to attempt to physically bring the fish out of the water with one strong effort and motion. He would simply, but stupidly, seek to get the fish immediately airborne with the unrealistic hope and expectation that the fish, once airborne, would fly through the air and land in our boat.

Obviously this could and would never happen – either in fishing or when impeaching. In all probability we would lose the fish, lose our bait and hook, snap our line and, most tragically, spill our Guinness. Obviously, we will have done something wrong.

As our two fishermen explain, the sport and joy of fishing is to be experienced in slowly bringing the fish in. This is what fishing is all about – this is what makes fishing fun.

Accepting this understanding of fishing we now know and accept we will bring the fish in slowly and with purpose. With what purpose? Well, obviously the fish being brought in slowly will be suffering, with the hook in its mouth. Does it want to fight against us and pull back? So be it. This only prolongs its suffering. In truth, for you, the trial lawyer, bringing the fish in slowly is one of, if not the most, pleasant and enjoyable parts of the trial. You are in control, and little can go wrong.

Actually, when impeaching, we accomplish two purposes in bringing the fish in slowly.

Always remember your objectives – you want the jury to believe the truth is found in the statement and not the "new version," and secondarily you want them to believe the fish made contrary statements. To this end you want to *exalt*, *enshrine*, and *extol* the impeaching statement. You want the impeaching statement to have all of the indicia of reliability and truthfulness, to appear to be coming "from the burning bush." This purpose is obviously important – indeed, your most important consideration and purpose.

Your second purpose in bringing the fish in slowly is to close the possible opportunities the fish might have to escape. When the fish sees the boat and the net it will become desperate and seek any way to get away. We can and will take these opportunities away from the fish.

Keeping in mind our fishing analogy, it is now time to go into the courtroom and with purpose reel the fish in slowly.

Q: "You saw a car?"
A: "Yes."
Q: "Green?"
A: "No, the car was red."

You have the deposition of the witness where he said the car was green. We are using a deposition to demonstrate the implementation of Rule 3; however, you can substitute whatever you would normally use – a 302 FBI statement, a statement to the police, or an oral statement to the bartender Murphy. Obviously, the statement to Murphy would limit what you can do to extol the statement and to close the potential methods of escape.

How do we start the impeachment? Our experience suggests most lawyers are not sure how to get started. Usually, they want to get to the contradiction without first extolling the statement and closing the possible places of escape.

We start with a *transition*. This is explained in detail in *MacCarthy on Cross-Examination*. Obviously, how to use the transition must and will be demonstrated. Every time we change the focus of the cross-examination we start by using a transition.

Q: "I want to ask you some questions about the official deposition you gave on June 10 of last year, you understand?"

This is the MacCarthy transition. Obviously, it would be slightly different depending on the source of the impeaching statement. In lieu of the term deposition, you might be using "the official police statement" or even "what you told Mr. Murphy."

A: "Yes."
Q: "You went to your attorney's office that day?"
A: "Yes."
Q: "You got there a little before 2:00 in the afternoon?"
A: "Yes."
Q: "You told the receptionist who you were?"

We are into telling our story, having said to our self the magic words "once upon a time." We are also getting the witness into the "yes" mode. Again, see *MacCarthy on Cross-Examination.*

A: "Yes."
Q: "She took you into a room?"
A: "Yes."
Q: "A conference-type room?"
A: "Yes."
Q: "The room had a large table?"
A: "Yes."
Q: "Chairs around the table?"
A: "Yes."
Q: "You saw your attorney?"
A: "Yes."

Q: "I was there?"
A: "Yes."
Q: "There was a woman there you did not know?"
A: "Yes."
Q: "But you knew why she was there?"
A: "Yes."
Q: "She had a little white machine?"
A: "Yes."
Q: "She was working that machine?"
A: "Yes."
Q: "She was typing what your attorney said?"
A: "Yes."
Q: "She was typing what I said?"
A: "Yes."
Q: "Most importantly, she was typing what you said?"
A: "Yes."
Q: "Let me ask you some questions about how you started your official deposition, you understand?"
A: "Yes."
Q: "You took an oath?"
A: "Yes."
Q: "An oath to tell the truth?"
A: "Yes."
Q: "Your attorney told you what you said would be important?"
A: "Yes."
Q: "Of course, you knew what you said would be important?"
A: "Yes."
Q: "Your attorney told you to tell the truth?"
A: "Yes."
Q: "You wanted to tell the truth?"
A: "Yes."
Q: "You did tell the truth?"
A: "Yes."
Q: "Your attorney told you to give all the details?"
A: "Yes."

Q: "Certainly all the important details?"
A: "Yes."
Q: "And you did give all the details?"
A: "Yes."
Q: "Your attorney told you people would rely on what you said?"
A: "Yes."
Q: "He told you he would rely on what you said?"
A: "Yes."
Q: "He told you I would rely on what you said?"
A: "Yes."
Q: "Most importantly, he told you a jury – this jury – would rely on what you said?"
A: "Yes."
Q: "You wanted everybody to rely upon what you said?"
A: "Yes."
Q: "You wanted to help?"
A: "Yes."
Q: "You wanted to do the best you could?"
A: "Yes."
Q: "This was important to you?"
A: "Yes."
Q: "You know it was important to everyone?"
A: "Yes."
Q: "You gave this official deposition two weeks after you saw the (terrible collision or accident)?"
A: "Yes."
Q: "When things were fresh in your mind?"
A: "Yes."
Q: "You know the importance of having things fresh in your mind?"
A: "Yes."
Q: "You know people can tend to forget things?"
A: "Yes."
Q: "People can tend to forget things not fresh in their mind?"
A: "Yes."

Q: "Your attorney told you if you did not understand a question not to answer it?"
A: "Yes."
Q: "He told you that if you did not understand a question, say so?"
A: "Yes."
Q: "And twice during your official deposition you did say you did not understand the question?"
A: "Yes."
Q: "That question was further explained to you?"
A: "Yes."
Q: "Only then did you answer that question?"
A: "Yes."
Q: "After your official deposition was over, you were satisfied?"
A: "Yes."
Q: "You were satisfied you had given all the important details?"
A: "Yes."
Q: "You were satisfied that everyone could rely on what you had said?"
A: "Yes."
Q: "I want to ask you what happened a couple of weeks after you gave your accurate deposition, you understand?"
A: "Yes."
Q: "You received an envelope in the mail?"
A: "Yes."
Q: "It was from your attorney?"
A: "Yes."
Q: "You opened the envelope?"
A: "Yes."
Q: "It had a letter from your lawyer?"
A: "Yes."
Q: "It also had a copy of your official deposition?"
A: "Yes."
Q: "The letter told you to read the deposition?"
A: "Yes."

Q: "To read it carefully?"
A: "Yes."
Q: "It told you to see if there were any mistakes?"
A: "Yes."
Q: "You were told it was important you correct any mistakes?"[13]
A: "Yes."
Q: "You did make two corrections?"
A: "Yes."
Q: "This was important to you?"
A: "Yes."
Q: "Only after making these two corrections did you return the official deposition?"
A: "Yes."
Q: "Before returning the deposition, you signed it?"
A: "Yes."
Q: "You were satisfied it was truthful?"
A: "Yes."
Q: "You were satisfied it was accurate?"
A: "Yes."
Q: "You were satisfied people could rely upon it?"

We have done much to extol the deposition statement. We constantly (looping) refer to it as the "official" deposition. We have created the word picture of the court reporter and her machine. We have stressed the fact that the witness was truthful, accurate, that he knew of the deposition's importance, and that he knew and wanted others, particularly the jury, to rely upon what he said. He understands the questions. He gave all the important details. He wanted to help. He "carefully" read the deposition and, as instructed, made the required changes.

He gave the deposition when the facts were fresh in his mind. What he said, particularly his accuracy, was important to him. He wanted the jury to be able to rely upon what he said in his "official" deposition.

---

[13]Some jurisdictions allow the witness to make corrections, others do not.

We have satisfied the requirements of Rule 3; we have brought the fish in slowly and have done so with the purpose of extolling the statement and closing doors that might be used to escape.[14]

[14]There are a few additional recurring issues that might come up when you are "reeling in the fish." They are correct in the following Addendum.

For police officers who have written a report (this can be modified for doctors or other witnesses that write reports as part of their jobs), the reeling-in of the fish above involves four areas, which are followed by sample statements to use.

The first area is to show that the police officer was *trained to write a good report.* "Before you became a police officer, you went to the police academy?" "You trained to be a good police officer?" "You took different courses to learn how to do your job properly?" "To make sure the guilty were convicted?" "And to make sure innocent citizens were not convicted?" "Most importantly, you took a course in writing official police reports?" "These reports were important?" "An important part of your job is writing official police reports?" "It is important your official police report be completed?" "It is important to be accurate?" "It is important to be truthful?" "You were taught the importance of accurate details?"

The second area is to show that without a good official police report, the officer might not have a good memory of what happened. "Official police reports are important because you do not know when a case will go to trial?" "Many cases do no go to trial immediately?" "Some do not go to trial for weeks, months, or even years?" "You use the official police report to help you remember what happened in a particular case?" "You use the official police report to distinguish one case from another?" "Your official police report is the only written record you have of a particular case?"

The third area is to demonstrate that the officer knew other people would reply on the report. "When you finish the official police report, you sign it?" "You sign it only after you determine it is (LOOP) *complete*, *accurate*, and *truthful*?" "You knew others would rely on it?" "You knew other people would make decisions based on your official police report?"

Finally, because of the first three areas (trained to be a good police officer, without a good report the officer may not remember, and the fact others would rely on the report), *the officer wrote a good report in this case.* "In this case you wrote a report?" "An official police report?" "When you wrote your official police report, you wanted to be a good police officer?" "You were (LOOP) *complete*, *accurate*, and *truthful*?" "You included all the important details?" "You typed the report when it was fresh in your mind?" "When you finished typing, you read and reviewed your official police report?" "You made any necessary corrections to be sure it was (LOOP) *complete*, *accurate*, and *truthful* and to make sure it included all the important details?" "After reading and reviewing the official police report, you signed it?"

The fish might wiggle off the hook by saying "there's no box for that on the report," or "there was not enough room on the report." While cross-examining a police officer, you will usually welcome these responses. This issue can be dealt with while reeling-in the fish. "There are lines on the police report?" "You fill them in?" "You decide what to put on those lines?" "As much as you want?" "Or as little as you want?" "Where what you need to write does not fit, you can use supplemental reports?" "There are no limits to the number of supplemental reports you can add?"

Reeling-in the fish when the witness is a lay witness might present other issues. "I forgot to tell them," "it was not important," or "they never asked." "The police asked about the person that robbed you?" "They asked you to describe the person that robbed you?"

(*continued*)

Fishing Rule 4
"Net the Fish"

Only one of the three of us went to law school a long time ago. So only one of us was taught and learned the Rule in *Queen Caroline's Case*: 129 Eng. Rep. 976, 2B & 286 (1820). If you want to know how old a lawyer is, or more accurately how long ago they went to law school, simply ask them if they have heard of the Rule in *Queen Caroline's Case*. If they heard of it, they went to law school long ago, before 1970.

Those who never learned the rule missed out on an interesting bit of English history.

The rule itself is simply, if not wisely, stated. When impeaching with an inconsistent statement, you must have the common decency to show or read the statement to the witness. This sounds simple enough. Simple enough except wisely the rule no longer exists. The Rule in *Queen Caroline's Case* was eliminated by the drafters of the Federal Rules of Evidence. FRE Rule 613(a): "In examining a witness concerning a prior statement made by the witness, whether written or not, the statement need not be shown nor its contents disclosed to the witness at that time, but on request the same shall be shown or disclosed to opposing counsel." Actually it was eliminated in England in 1854, following much criticism by the bar.

Although the rule was ostensibly abolished, the courts have not always fully agreed with its abolishment. In *United States v. Marks*, 81B F.2d 1207 (7th Cir. 1987), the court, affirming a criminal conviction, found there to be no error in the trial judge requiring defense counsel to show the

---

(footnote continued from previous page)
"They told you to tell them everything you could remember?" "To give as many details as possible?" "To tell them any distinguishing characteristics – distinctive features – anything that stood out about clothing – face – appearance?" "To tell them anything they could use to find the person that did this?" "This was shortly after the robbery?" "The robbery was fresh in your mind?" "You wanted to catch the offender?" "You knew they would rely on what you told them?" "You wanted them to rely on what you told them?" "You knew what you told them was important?" "You wanted to help their investigation as best you could?" "You wanted justice?" "You knew this was a serious case?" "You wanted to do everything you could to help the police?" "You told them the truth?" "You were (LOOP) *complete*, *accurate*, and *truthful*?" "So they could catch your robber?" "So you described the robber?" "Told them everything you could remember?" "You gave as many details as possible – as many distinguishing characteristics as possible – because you knew . . . (LOOP some of the above)?"

impeaching statement to the witness. In a word, the trial judge can ". . .in particular circumstances. . ." require the *Queen Caroline Case* approach.

Also, in *Soloman v. Tadlock*, 21 F.3d 1462 (9th Cir. 1994), the Ninth Circuit held the "appropriate manner" was to require the statement be shown to the witness.

Though interesting, these cases that require adherence to the Rule in *Queen Caroline's Case* will pose no problems to us. We will abide by and follow the rule. We will do so not merely because a few courts may require us to do so, and not merely because failure to follow the rule may preclude us from introducing the extrinsic evidence (the statement) necessary to "kill the fish";[15] we will follow the rule because usually it is the better trial procedure. It makes us, as trial lawyers, appear fairer and more prepared.

So then we, in obedience to Fishing Rule 4, "net the fish" by showing the fish the impeaching statement.

Now a slight diversion. How do we show a witness a statement: any and all witnesses and any and all statements? Yes, we are going back to Trial Advocacy 101.

In showing a witness a statement many lawyers, as they were taught and what they have seen others do, use some version of the following language. "Mr. Witness, I now show you what has been previously marked as defense exhibit three for identification, which purports to be the deposition you gave on or about April 1 of 2012, and I ask you sir, do you recognize it?"

This is horrible. In the first place, it totally violates MacCarthy Trial Advocacy Rule 11, which requires we speak in a courtroom the way we would speak in a bar.

Second, this is terrible direct examination, and it is even worse if it is a cross, as it does not use a statement, but a question.

Third, and finally, this "legal speak" is stupid for the following reasons:

- Why tell everyone you are showing the witness something when they can obviously see you are doing just that?

[15]FRE 613(b): "Extrinsic evidence of a prior inconsistent statement by a witness is not admissible unless the witness is afforded an opportunity to explain or deny the same and the opposite party is afforded the opportunity to interrogate the witness thereon, or the interests of justice otherwise require."

- The term "previously marked" makes no sense. Anything that was marked was marked before.
- Do you really need the qualifying language "for identification?" We think not.
- Telling the witness what the exhibit "purports to be" would be improper on direct examination and not the way to cross-examine.
- "Do you recognize it," obviously a question, is big-time legal speak. If this is direct examination, ask the simple question: "Do you know what this is?" If cross-examination, simply say "You know what this is?"

How then do we show a witness a document? Going back to where we started, we will "net the fish into a boat" and use an example of impeachment with an inconsistent statement. Actually, the example we use is of little or no importance; we will use the same process whenever we show a witness a document.

We will follow three steps.

Step One

"Your Honor, may I show the witness defense exhibit three?"

As trial lawyers this is not something we do to help our cause. Nonetheless, we do it because it is required. The court of appeals, in reading the record, will want to know what exhibit we are using. Besides, many trial judges want you to seek permission to approach the witness, and it shows proper manners.

Step Two

"Counsel, (addressing your opponent) defense exhibit three, page eleven, lines fourteen and fifteen." This is not a necessary step, but it is a good one, as will be explained.

Make sure you have followed the legal, *no less*, the civility requirements. In a word, make sure your opponent has a copy of defense exhibit three. Contrast this to the trial of O.J. Simpson. More times than not the other side, be it prosecution or defense, would interrupt the showing of a document (no, they did not follow the Step Two procedure) to a witness with an objection that they did not have a copy of the document. Apart from legal and civility considerations, the lawyer using the document does not want their presentation interrupted by proper objections.

If you are using a deposition, the lines will be numbered. On most other documents you will have to mark the lines – obviously something you must and will do in advance.

Do you then give your opponent a copy with your premarked lines? Civility need not extend that far. It is interesting to see how long your opponent spends deciding which are lines fourteen and fifteen.

From a trial advocacy perspective, following Step Two looks good. You are being fair and considerate to your opponent, though in truth they would just as soon you not be so "fair and considerate."

So also, the witness cannot help but notice your "letting the air out" of their lawyer. And, particularly if this procedure is repeated, the jury will anticipate and usually look forward to the impeachment.

How can you be sure you want to follow this Step Two procedure? Following it will occasionally produce an objection – your opponent does not like what you are doing to them. At best the objection, which will be summarily overruled, will come in the form of "Your Honor, I object, Counsel is talking to me!"

Step Three

Approaching the witness: "You know what this is?"

After the witness gives their brief affirmation "yes" answer, you follow up by telling the witness and the jury "what it is." "This is your official deposition?"[16]

Now select three good ones from what you did bringing the fish in.

"This is the official deposition where you told the truth."

"This is the official deposition where you told us all of the important facts."

"This is the official deposition you wanted this jury to rely upon?"

The fish is in the boat ready to be executed.

[16]Obviously if this occurred on direct examination, you would use a question: "Do you know what this is?"

Fishing Rule 5
"Kill The Fish"

You now have the fish in the boat. You have the fish midboat and you place your right foot midfish. Your gloved left hand has pliers to be used in pulling out, with no concern for the comfort of the fish, the hook. You are now ready to all but kill the fish. Yes, now you may put down your Guinness. The sport has ended.

Obviously you will use the inconsistent statement. The trial advocacy issue is raised – who will read the statement? Should the fish read the statement? It looks like the fairer way to do it. Also, the contrary statements will come out of the same mouth.

But you know how the statement will come out of the fish's mouth – not articulated well and with absolutely no emphasis. To accomplish the preferred articulation and trial advocacy emphasis you will have to be the one to read the statement.

Which option do you prefer? Actually, you need not make this choice. There is a third option, and it is the better option. Do it both ways. Have the fish read the statement to show fairness and have the contrary statement come from the mouth of the fish. Then you repeat the statement with the gusto of a communicative trial lawyer.

Let us do it.

Q: "Please read to the jury what you said you saw when you left Murphy's bar?"
A: "I saw a green car."
Q: "You said you knew the driver of the green car?"[17]
A: "Yes."
Q: "You said Clancy was driving the *green car*?"
A: "Yes."
Q: "You said the *green car* was going west?"
A: "Yes."

You also may wish to consider writing "green car" on the blackboard. You have all but killed the fish.

---

[17] We "loop" the *green* car three times.

As a word of caution, this is not the time to "publish" or move the impeaching statement into evidence. Wait to do this until you have completed your cross-examination. Then, and only then, will it be time to move the impeaching statement into evidence and "publish" (translated: show) the impeaching statement to the jury.

If you show the jurors the impeaching statement during your cross-examination they will understandably start to look at it – during your cross-examination. You do not want this. Better they should read it after you have completed your cross-examination, or even better during your opponent's redirect examination.

Some Problems

There will be times when the fish will not allow you to kill it.

Recall the "collateral" problem that could arise when impeaching with an inconsistent statement. The issue is not important and is therefore collateral. You will not then be able to introduce the "extrinsic" evidence; the inconsistent statement.

This could certainly limit what you can do. To alleviate, at least in part, this problem you should use the "persuasive document" as explained under the topic Truthfulness Impeachment.

Still another problem could arise.

Q: "Would you read to the jury what you saw when you left Murphy's Bar?"

A: "Well what you handed me says I saw a green car, but that is not what I said. I told them I saw a red car."

The fish will not let you kill it. You cannot be the one to kill the fish during your cross-examination. The killing will be done, but it will be delayed and someone else will have to do the killing. Worry not – you will still not only observe the killing, but also be much involved with your right foot midfish.

So let us bring in someone else to kill the fish. The fish killer will be a witness you will call on direct examination. It will be one who was present when the fish made the impeaching statement. Using our deposition situation it will probably be the court reporter. In a criminal case it will often be the law enforcement agent who took the impeaching statement. Imagine, if you would, a criminal case in the federal court. The impeaching statement may well be an FBI 302, the statement taken by the FBI from a witness. Given this situation, the honor of killing the fish goes to Special Agent Efrem Zimbalist, Jr. Think of it. He will be your witness. It is your friendly arm over his shoulder as you lead him to the witness stand. After a few pleasant introductory questions which tell a bit about what he does at Quantico, Virginia, you allow him to be the one to kill the fish. Remember this is direct and not cross-examination.

Q: "Did you talk to Perjuring Pete?"
A: "Yes I did."
Q: "I want to ask you some questions about the Official FBI statement you took from Perjuring Pete on June 10 of 2013, do you understand?"
A: "Yes."
Q: "Who else was with you when you took this statement?"
A: "Special Agent Jones."
Q: "Was this an *official* statement?"
A: "Yes."
Q: "Was this *official* statement what you call a 302 statement?"
A: "Yes it was."
Q: "Did you explain the importance of this *official* statement to Perjuring Pete?"
A: "Yes we did."
Q: "Did you tell him it was important he tell the truth?"
A: "Yes we did."
Q: "Did you tell him to tell you all of the facts, all of the details?"
A: "Yes."
Q: "Did you tell him the FBI would rely on what he said?"
A: "I do not recall telling him strictly that."
Q: "But you wanted to be able to rely on what he told you."
A: "Yes."

Q: "You took this *official* FBI statement no less than a week after the bank robbery?"

A: "Yes."

Q: "When the details would have been relatively fresh in his mind?"

A: "Yes."

Q: "Did you and Special Agent Jones ask Perjuring Pete questions?"

A: "Yes we did."

Q: "Were these questions important to you?"

A: "Yes."

Q: "Likewise, would the answers have been of importance to you?"

A: "Yes, they would have."

Q: "Did you or Special Agent Jones tell Perjuring Pete that if he did not understand any of your questions he should let you know?"

A: "Yes, we did."

Q: "Did he ever tell you he did not understand any of your questions?"

A: "No."

Q: "At any time did he appear to you as not having understood your questions?"

A: "No."

Q: "I want to ask you some questions about what he told you he saw when he left Murphy's Bar, do you understand?"

A: "Ok."

Q: "Were these answers important to you?"

A: "All of his answers were important to us."

Q: "What he did in Murphy's Bar was not particularly important to you, was it?"

A: "No, not really."

Q: "And what he saw and did an hour after he left Murphy's Bar was not particularly important to you, was it?"

A: "Not really."

Q: "Would it be fair to say that what was important to you was what he saw when he left Murphy's Bar."

A: "Yes."

Q: "Did you write down what he told you he saw when he left Murphy's Bar?"

A: "Yes."

Q: "Were you careful to make sure you wrote down his facts accurately?"

A: "Yes."

Q: "I want to ask you some questions about what he told you he saw when he left Murphy's Bar, do you understand?"

A: "Yes."

Q: "What did he tell you he saw?"

A: "A car."

Q: "What did he tell you was the make of the car?"

A: "A Pontiac."

Q: "Did you ask him what color the Pontiac was?"

A: "Yes we did."

Q: "And did he tell you the color of the Pontiac?"

A: "Yes, he did."

Q: "Would you tell the ladies and gentlemen of the jury what color he told you the car he saw was?"

A: "Green."

Q: "Who did he tell you was driving the *green* car?"

A: "Tom Clancy."

Q: "Did he tell you if there was a passenger in the green car he saw?"

A: "Yes. He said there was a blonde woman he did not know in the passenger seat."

Q: "Did he tell you what direction the *green* car he saw was going?"

A: "Yes. He said it was going West."

*Write "Green Car" on the blackboard

Q: "Did you accurately write down all of this information in your official FBI report?"

A: "Yes."

Q: "Did you specifically and accurately write down the color of the car he saw?"

A: "Yes."

Q: "What did you write down in your official FBI report was the color of the car he saw?"

A: "Green."

The Special Agent has done an excellent job of killing the fish for you.

The Second Time Around

Usually, once you have properly and thoroughly impeached a witness (fish) with an inconsistent statement, the fish, or now if you prefer the puppy, will have received the message.[18] The severity of the punishment will help put and keep the witness in the "yes" mode. They should now understand that it is much better, easier, and less painful to simply answer all of your statements with a simple "yes." This makes sense, but what should happen if the fish did not get or understand the first message?

Obviously, "the second time around" all of the Fishing Rules apply – but some less so than the first time. Fishing Rules 1 and 2 fully apply. Fishing Rule 3 requires a major adjustment.

Recall, a trial lawyer should not be in the business of boring jurors. Were we to "bring the fish in slowly" a second time, this would bore the jury. You do not want to try to suddenly yank the fish in the boat, but, on the other hand, you must get it there much sooner than the first time.

You will have already "exalted" the impeaching statement and will have closed the possible escape areas. There is no need to do this again, unless of course you are using a different statement. There is no need to tell your "once upon a time" story again.

So how will we do "the second time around" impeachment?

Q: "You saw a fire truck?"

A: "No, I saw a bread truck."

---

[18] You will have punished the fish by hitting it in the head with a baseball bat.

Q: "I want to again ask you some questions about the official deposition you gave on June 10, 2013, you understand?"

A: "Yes."

Now Select Three Good Ones

Q: "That was your truthful official deposition statement?"

A: "Yes."

Q: "That is the official deposition statement you wanted this jury to rely upon?"

A: "Yes."

Q: "This is the official deposition statement you gave when everything was *fresh in your mind*?"

A: "Yes."

You have completed Fishing Rule 3 Go to Fishing Rule 4 and then 5

"Your Honor, may I once again show the witness (do not call him a 'fish') defense exhibit three?"

Returning to Fishing Rules 4 and 5, you can repeat a few good points preferably three, that is, accurate, truthful, fresh in mind, knew it was important, wanted jury to rely on.

When you have all but killed the fish and when you have completed your cross-examination you may, and should, move to have the inconsistent statement admitted into evidence. If the statement was made under oath, request the judge instruct the jury that the statement comes in not merely to impeach but as substantive evidence.[19]

---

[19]"The inconsistent statement exhibit should be admitted into evidence as being the best evidence of the contradiction, even though the witness admits making the consistent statement." *Gordon v. United States*, 344 U.S. 414, 420–21 (1953).

"Where a witness denies or cannot recall a prior inconsistent statement, that statement may be read to the jury for impeachment." *United States v. Dennis*, 625 F.2d 782, 796 (8th Cir. 1980).

See also United States v. Lee, 867 F.2d 206, 208 (4th Cir. 1989) (the terms of the plea agreement between the government and its witness, including a grant of formal immunity, were used to impeach the witness and were then read to the jury); *Lentomyynti Oy v.*

(*continued*)

Fishing Rule 6
"Do Not Play with the Almost-Dead Fish"

Rule 6 properly suggests that once you have completed your impeachment, you move on. To "play with the fish" you have to put your Guinness down – that fact alone should assure you will never "play with the fish." Besides, do you really want to hold a stinky, slimy, bloody, half-dead fish? In holding and playing with the fish you are inviting a possible disaster. You may lose hold of the fish, and it might fall back in the lake where, at worst, it may recover and, in any event, you no longer have the fish to eat.

Usually this rule presents few problems. But the rule has been violated.

When trying his first case, the youngest of our three authors did an outstanding job cross-examining the main prosecution witness. The opportunity was presented to impeach the main witness with an inconsistent statement. Fishing Rules 1 through 5 were followed exceptionally well. With consummate skill the fish was killed.

Then, for an unexplainable reason, Rule 6 was violated, for that matter, as often follows, the basic rules of cross-examination were violated with, for example, "Is your memory better now than it was then?" The other Rule 6 violations were at least done with proper cross-examination style.

They rehashed a few of the points made in "bringing the fish in."

Fortunately, this mistake did not doom the result. The criminal defendant was found not guilty.[20]

(footnote continued from previous page)
Medivac, Inc., 887 F.2d 364, 373 (7th Cir. 1993) (defendant used inconsistent statements to impeach plaintiffs' witness and read the statements to the jury during cross-examination.)

[20]The more acute minds raise the proper question, "how do you know all of this?" When defense lawyers get a not guilty, they do not get a transcript.

Being his first jury trial, his supervisor, Bill Ward an outstanding trial lawyer and now the Public Defender in Minneapolis, Minnesota, was kind enough to have the all-important cross-examination, which had impressed everyone, transcribed so they could give a copy to his proud father.

CHAPTER 2
Contradictions

Again, one could make the argument that contradiction impeachment does not deserve this high a rating, partially because trial lawyers are not all that familiar with contradiction impeachment and, even more significantly, because the opportunities to use contradiction impeachment do not arise all that often – particularly when compared to inconsistent statement impeachment. Also, it is somewhat related to, indeed sometimes confused with, inconsistent statement impeachment. This is a good time to consider it. Something had to be rated second, and this seems like a good, if not perfect, choice.

Its impact score is relatively high, actually higher than the inconsistent statement impact score. Someone else, hopefully a highly respected someone else, is telling the jury that the witness is either mistaken or, more probably, lying. It usually has an evidentiary limitation, the same "collateral" limitation as in inconsistent statement impeachment.

Contradiction impeachment is not spelled out in the Federal Rules of Evidence. Although somewhat like motivation impeachment, some would desire to give it a "home" in the Federal Rules of Evidence. A few courts have suggested its "home" is FRE 607.[21]

[21]"Rule 607 of the Federal Rules of Evidence – authorizes impeachment by contradiction, and Rule 403 governs its application." *U.S. v. Gilmore*, 553 F.3d 266 (3d Cir. 2009).

As discussed earlier, Fed. R. Evid. 607 spells out your right to impeach your own witness. This may be a bit of a stretch in an effort to give contradiction impeachment a "home." Actually, as with motivation impeachment, its common law heritages should be sufficient. Then again, giving it a "home," however questionable, creates no problems.

Contradiction impeachment can be, and often is, confused with inconsistent statement impeachment, with truthfulness impeachment, and with capacity impeachment. Yet it has its own uniqueness.[22]

You have evidence that contradicts, is contrary, to something the witness has said either on direct or cross-examination.

If the witness tells the bartender at Murphy's Bar that he just saw a green car, but while testifying tells us the car was red, you should impeach with an inconsistent statement. Then again, there are those who would argue that this is contradiction impeachment. Do whatever, the method you use will make little difference.

A few obvious examples of contradiction impeachment might prove helpful.

- The witness testifies he worked on March 17. You have his time card from the factory, and he neither punched in nor punched out on that day.
- He testifies it was a very cold day. You have the day's weather report which shows the temperature was in the seventies. (You would be following in the footsteps of Abraham Lincoln.)
- He testifies he never left his home all day. You have witnesses who saw him in Murphy's restaurant and a copy of the credit card bill he signed.

This impeachment may be started on cross-examination, though most probably it will await your direct examination where your witness or evidence will contradict the earlier testimony.

---

[22] *U.S. v. Collicott*, 92 F. 3d 980 n.5 (9th Cir. 1996)

Recall the "collateral" evidence restriction that applies to inconsistent statement impeachment. Though, as earlier suggested, this restriction makes little sense, in all probability it will be applied to your contradiction impeachment. Accepting this, you will want to read about "the persuasive document" and "the phantom document" under truthfulness impeachment.

Note the use of the terms "in all probability." Proudly we tell you that there are courts, unfortunately few, and commentators who would not apply the "collateral" limitation to contradiction impeachment. Though we commend them, it is difficult to see how they can make this distinction and reach this conclusion.[23]

Contradiction impeachment is, as most all else, subject to Rule 403. The probative value of your impeachment must substantially outweigh any unfair prejudice. So also the other Rule 403 restrictions apply; confusion of the issues, misleading the jury, undue delay, waste of time, or needless cumulative evidence.

A reading of the case law suggests that contradiction impeachment is best understood and used by prosecutors. They use it to impeach defendants who testify.[24]

Go back to our discussion of inconsistent statement impeachment, more specifically the "what is a statement" issue. We suggested that a few judges give a narrow interpretation to what is a statement of the witness. We used the FBI 302 statement as a possible example. We suggested that a judge's decision to not allow you to impeach with an inconsistent statement – having decided that it is not the witness's statement – will not only present no problems, but rather will improve your "impact score" and your impeachment.

---

[23]See McCormick on Evidence § 47 at 112 n.20 (Edward W. Cleary et al. eds., 3d ed. 1984) ("Cases suggesting that even if "collateral" the judge has discretion to permit the contradiction. *Salem News Co. v. Caliga*, 144 F. 965 (1st Cir. 1906); *Todd v. Bradley*, 99 Conn. 307, 122 A. 68 (1923); *Lizotte v. Warren*, 302 Mass. 317, 19 N.E.2d 60 (1939) (self-contradiction by party)").

[24]*United States v. Gilmore*, 553 F. 3d 266 (3d Cir. 2009).

We suggest you cross as follows:

Q: "I want to ask you some questions about what you told the FBI agents on June 10 of this year, you understand?"[25]
A: "Ok."
Q: "You knew this was an important investigation?"
A: "Yes."
Q: "You wanted to cooperate?"
A: "Yes."
Q: "You wanted to help the FBI?"
A: "Yes."
Q: "They asked you to be truthful?"
A: "Yes."
Q: "You wanted to be truthful?"
A: "Yes."
Q: "You were truthful?"
A: "Yes."
Q: "They asked you to give them accurate information?"
A: "Yes."
Q: "You wanted to give them accurate information?"
A: "Yes."
Q: "You did give them accurate information?"
A: "Yes."
Q: "You talked to them two days after you had been in Murphy's Bar?"
A: "Yes."
Q: "When things were still fresh in your mind?"
A: "Yes."
Q: "You knew the importance of things being fresh in your mind?"
A: "Yes."
Q: "We can all forget things not fresh in our minds?"
A: "Yes."
Q: "The agents asked you questions?"
A: "Yes."

[25]Fishing Rule 3 explains this in greater detail.

Q: "They told you if you did not understand any of their questions to let them know?"
A: "Yes."
Q: "You did not have to 'let them know?'"
A: "Yes."
Q: "You understood their questions?"
A: "Yes."
Q: "They wanted to know what you saw when you left the bar?"
A: "Yes."
Q: "You knew this was important to them?"
A: "Yes."
Q: "You told them you saw a car?"
A: "Yes."
Q: "They wanted to know the color of the car?"
A: "Yes."
Q: "Again, you knew this was important to them?"
A: "Yes."
Q: "You told them the color of the car you saw?"
A: "Yes."
Q: "You told them it was green?"
A: "No, I told them it was red."
Q: "Now, under oath, you are telling our jury you told the FBI Special Agents the car was red?"
A: "Yes."
Q: "Again, under oath, you deny telling the FBI Special Agents the car you saw was green?"
A: "Yes."

Obviously, you have not impeached the witness with an inconsistent statement, because the judge has ruled that the 302 statement is not the witness's statement. In a word, the judge will not let you impeach with an inconsistent statement.

Actually, you will profit from having to change your method of impeachment. Now it will not be you, but rather one or two Special Agents, who will call him a liar.

Direct Examination

Using our example you get to put a witness on the stand, an FBI Special Agent, or maybe two, no less. You get to do the preliminaries to the direct examination: who he is and what he does.

Q: "Were you the Special Agent in charge of this investigation?"
A: "Yes."
Q: "Did you talk to Mr. Smith?"
A: "Yes."
Q: "Where did you talk to him?"
A: "At our FBI office."
Q: "Who else was there?"
A: "Special Agent Jones."
Q: "When was this?"
A: "June 10 of this year."
Q: "Did you take an official FBI statement?"
A: "Yes."
Q: "What do you call that statement?"
A: "A 302 statement."
Q: "Was this official 302 statement important to you?"
A: "Yes."
Q: "Did you explain this to Mr. Smith?"
A: "Yes."
Q: "Did you tell him you wanted him to be truthful?"
A: "Yes, we did."
Q: "Did he tell you he would be truthful?"
A: "Yes."
Q: "Did you explain to him the importance of him giving you accurate facts?"
A: "Yes, we did."
Q: "Did you tell him you would rely on his answers?"
A: "Yes."
Q: "Did you tell him that the U.S. Attorney's Office would rely on his answers?"
A: "Yes."

Q: "Did you tell him a jury would rely on the accuracy and truthfulness of his facts?"
A: "I do not know if we told him this."
Q: "Let me ask you some questions about the questions you asked and the answers he gave about what he saw when he left Murphy's Bar, do you understand?"
A: "Yes."
Q: "You were particularly interested in knowing what he saw when he left Murphy's Bar?"
A: "Yes, that was important to us."
Q: "More specifically, did you want to know the color of the car he saw?"
A: "Yes, this was important to us."
Q: "Did you ask him the color of the car he saw?"
A: "Yes, we did."
Q: "Did he answer this question?"
A: "Yes."
Q: "Did you in some way record his answer?"
A: "Yes, I wrote it down."
Q: "Did you write it down in your Official FBI 302 statement?"
A: "Yes."
Q: "Do you remember the color of the car he saw?"
A: "Yes, I do."
Q: "Did you check your Official FBI 302 statement to double check what he told you was the color of the car he saw?"
A: "Yes, I do not think this was necessary, but I did."
Q: "Was it necessary?"
A: "No it was not, both my memory and the 302 were the same."
Q: "Special Agent Black, would you please tell the jury what color Mr. Smith said the car he saw was?"
A: "He said it was green."
Q: "Is there any question in your mind about this?"
A: "No, there is not."
Q: "Are you sure he did not tell you the car was red?"
A: "Yes, I am."

Many will be tempted to do even more to "play with the fish," even though the "fish" is not on the stand, though most judges will not allow it.

> Q: "If Mr. Smith, under oath, told this jury that he told you the car he saw was red, would he have been correct?"
> A: "No."
> Q: "Would he have been either mistaken or lying?"
> A: "Yes he would."

No doubt the best known and most frequently referenced contradiction impeachment was done by no less that Abraham Lincoln. His 1857 defense of William "Duff" Armstrong resulted in what is often referred to as the *Almanac Trial.*

Armstrong's father was a good friend of Lincoln from his time in Salem. They had served together in the Black Hawk War. Lincoln took the murder case pro bono. Though a good trial lawyer, Lincoln had only won one of the five murder cases he had tried.

A co-defendant had already been convicted. Armstrong's trial was held in May in Beardstown. The main prosecution witness testified he clearly saw the fight and murder. Lincoln's cross put into question the witness's ability to see some distance across a field. To buttress his story, the witness explained there was a full moon.

To contradict the witness, Lincoln used an almanac to show there was no full moon that evening.

After an hour of deliberation, the jury acquitted Armstrong.

CHAPTER 3

Motivation

Motivation is the term we use to identify this important method of impeachment. It is also the term used by the United States Supreme Court in the leading case of *Davis v. Alaska*, 415 U.S. 308 (1974). Many, particularly criminal defense lawyers and prosecutors, simply call this method of impeachment "bias and prejudice" impeachment.

Obviously this method of impeachment would include "bias and prejudice," but a more extensive description would be helpful and possibly necessary. A witness with any animus, any interest, any reason, well founded or not, to favor one party or disfavor one party, or any reason to color their testimony to help or hurt a party, could be subjected to his form of impeachment. The more inclusive term would be "motive," and thus, we will label this form of impeachment "motivation" impeachment.

Some legal discussions of this form of impeachment suggest the motive (our term) must be an "irrational" one. This is obviously incorrect. The reason, or absence thereof, for the motive is totally unimportant. In a word, it could be totally "irrational" or totally "rational," but still be used to impeach.

We have elevated this form of impeachment to a high level of importance, indeed one of the most important of the sixteen ways to impeach. An argument could be made, certainly by civil trial lawyers, that motivation impeachment does not deserve this high a rating. We resolved the issue by voting on it. In that two of us are, more accurately, one was before becoming a judge, criminal trial lawyers, and only one is a civil trial lawyer; the vote was two to one to keep motivation impeachment where we have it. Besides, the United States Supreme Court apparently agrees with us. It is a more favored form of impeachment as compared with the "less favored forms of impeachment." *U.S. v. Abel*, 469 U.S. 45, 52 (1984).

Applying our criteria, we have scored motivation impeachment as follows:

Frequency of Use:	[7] Next only to inconsistent statement impeachment and contradiction impeachment.
Impact:	[4] This usually has a low impact score. We are not proving the witness to be a liar or even to be mistaken. Rather, we are making an issue as to the witness's reliability. We are merely showing the witness has a reason to color their testimony. However, motivation impeachment has a great potential for "bonus points." Bonus points, to be later explained, have high impact scores.
Limitations:	[10] As we shall see, there are few, if any evidentiary limitations on motivation impeachment.

With these scores, motivation impeachment deserves a high rating. Though, again, civil lawyers properly question this.

Motivation impeachment is, for the most part, unique among the major methods of impeachment in that it is not spelled out in its own Federal Rule of Evidence. It is not ignored in that it is mentioned in the commentary to Federal Rules of Evidence 401, 607, 608, and 611(b). But, as with contradiction and capacity impeachment, it is a major method of impeachment without its own Federal Rule of Evidence.

That it does not have its own rule is no problem. It has a common law background, and the courts have done an excellent job of interpreting, though not always recognizing, motivation impeachment. The courts also do an excellent job with jury instructions related to motivation impeachment.

A few states, Indiana comes to mind, have attempted to codify motivation impeachment into a specific rule of evidence.[26]

The common law origins of motivation impeachment is best understood in appreciating that at early common law, witnesses with any interest (motivation) in a case were ineligible to testify as witnesses. Obviously this created major problems and made little sense. Wisely, this disqualification was eliminated. To compensate for eliminating the disqualification, witnesses with interest (motivation) could be impeached on the basis of this interest (motivation) by the opposing attorney. This made much sense.

The Trilogy of Cases

Three decisions of the United States Supreme Court serve to best explain and define motivation impeachment. Obviously, these were not the first Supreme Court cases to recognize and talk about motivation impeachment, but read together they tell us essentially what we want to know about the law of motivation impeachment.

Davis v. Alaska, 415 U.S. 308 (1974).

This is the leading and most significant case. It is the best case for recognizing, enunciating, and liberally interpreting the use of motivation impeachment.

The facts of this Alaska criminal case are simple. The criminal defense lawyer commendably sought to impeach a prosecution witness by having him admit he was on probation, which made him subject to some control by the prosecution. The trial judge would not allow the impeachment, relying on a state statute that protected the anonymity of defendants convicted of misdemeanor crimes. The appeal found its way all the way up to the United States Supreme Court.

The conviction was reversed and remanded. The trial judge, said the Supreme Court, committed reversible error in not allowing the defense attorney to perfect his motivation impeachment. More specifically the opinion, authored by Chief Justice Warren Burger, said, "We have recognized that the exposure of a witness' motivation in testifying is a proper

[26]Indiana Rules of Court - Rules of Evidence, Rule 616. Witness's Bias: "Evidence that a witness has a bias, prejudice, or interest for or against any party may be used to attack the credibility of the witness."

and important function of the constitutionally protected right of cross-examination." *Davis v. Alaska*, 415 U.S. 308, 316 (1974).

Obviously the attempted impeachment was proper motivation impeachment, though in truth its impact may not have been particularly strong.

As spelled out by the Chief Justice, the defendant's right in *Davis* comes from the confrontation clause. Notwithstanding, prosecutors and civil trial lawyers, as will be explained, have the right to use proper motivation impeachment.

The opinion also holds that the appeal is subject to de novo review and not merely review for "plain error."

United States v. Abel, 469 U.S. 45 (1984) is the second significant case. *Abel* was tried in the federal court for a savings and loan robbery. The defense put on a witness named Mills to help the defendant's case. Mills testified Ehle, who was involved in the robbery, had told him he was going to lie about Abel's involvement to help himself.

In cross-examining Mills the Assistant United States Attorney, obviously aware of motivation impeachment, commendably sought to and did use it.

He crossed Mills about the fact that when he and the defendant had been in prison together (bonus points) they were both members of a secret gang or society. The trial judge would not allow the secret society to be identified as the Aryan Brotherhood. One of the tenets of their secret society was they would lie to help a fellow member. It sounded like appropriate motivation impeachment and, more importantly, it sounded like appropriate motivation impeachment to the trial judge.

The witness, obviously not wanting to be impeached, and also obeying the gang tenet to always deny the existence of the gang, denied the existence of the "secret society" and its tenets.

Again, the prosecutor showed his mastery of motivation impeachment and, in so doing, created an issue for the Ninth Circuit Court of Appeals. The prosecutor's rebuttal evidence included witnesses who supported the motivation impeachment by testifying that both Mills and the defendant, when in prison together, were members of the gang or secret society, and that one of its tenets was to lie for each other.

Through the use of extrinsic evidence the motivation impeachment was perfected; significantly, the "impact" score was greatly enhanced by "bonus points." Not only did the witness have a reason to color his testimony and, for that matter, to lie, but he had in fact lied when he denied membership in the secret society and the tenet requiring lying for fellow members.

This was excellent trial advocacy and yet it led to the argument advanced by the defense in the appeal. Their concerns were with the use of extrinsic evidence, and in particular the resulting "bonus points" – including the description of the secret society and its "lie to help" tenet.

The defense attorneys argued to the Ninth Circuit, as they had to the trial judge, that the prosecutor should have been stuck with the witness's answers. The exceptionally damaging extrinsic evidence, in the form of the rebuttal witnesses, should not have been allowed.

The Ninth Circuit accepted this argument and reversed the conviction. *United States v. Abel*, 707 F.2d 1013 (9th Cir. 1983). The Supreme Court reversed, holding that extrinsic evidence can be used to perfect motivation impeachment.

It is no wonder we are often confused by the evidentiary restrictions imposed on impeachment. We have learned that inconsistent statement impeachment can be, under certain circumstances, limited by the "collateral" rule. We also learned that most judges will similarly limit contradiction impeachment by the "collateral" rule. Now we learn that motivation impeachment is *not* limited by the "collateral" rule. Next we will learn that truthfulness impeachment will *always* be limited by the "collateral" rule. Again, we would be better served if the "collateral" rule, dedicated to "speed" and not to getting to the truth, were to be abolished.

Abel teaches us *all* trial lawyers may use motivation impeachment, though unlike the criminal defense lawyer the right is not a constitutional one. We also know motivation impeachment is not limited by the "collateral" rule. And finally, we see how little we need to use motivation impeachment and how we might be allowed to develop "bonus" points. ("Bonus" points is further explained later.)

Of historical interest, the *Abel* case involved several prominent attorneys, judges, and two eventual Supreme Court Justices.

Then judge, and now Justice Kennedy, dissented in the Ninth Circuit. Ninth Circuit judge Steven Trott, then an assistant Attorney General, argued the case for the prosecution in the Supreme Court. With him on the brief was now Supreme Court Justice Samuel A. Alito, Jr.

Delaware v. Van Arsdale, 475 U.S. 673 (1986) completes our trilogy of cases. The lawyering and indeed the judging in this case leaves much to be desired. The result is a confusing, complex, and convoluted case history.

Simply stated, we had a murder trial in the Delaware state courts. The defense attorney sought to impeach a prosecution witness with motivation impeachment. He attempted to show a prosecution witness had been charged with a "public drunkenness" misdemeanor that the prosecution dismissed. To say the least, the prosecutor and trial judge overreacted. The prosecutor objected to the impeachment. More surprisingly, the trial judge sustained the objection. It is difficult to imagine any support for the objection, nor to understand why the objection was sustained.

Following *Davis v. Alaska*, the case should have been summarily reversed and the Delaware Supreme Court did just that.

Unfortunately the facts strongly suggest another potential issue. The witness was, at best, redundant. His testimony was totally unnecessary. It placed the defendant in the same room with the murdered woman shortly before she was murdered. That might have been important except for the fact that the defendant agreed he was in the room with the murdered woman shortly before she was murdered.

Thus, we have a meaningless witness who the trial judge would not allow to be properly impeached with motivation impeachment.

Unfortunately, from these twisted and convoluted facts, we have the potential for the application of the "harmless error" rule to motivation impeachment.

Being honest and fair, if ever the "harmless error" rule should apply to a fact situation, this fact situation would be it. Then again, do we really want to compromise the constitutional right to properly confront witnesses with motivation impeachment with the, at best, questionable "harmless error" rule?

This was the problem that faced the Delaware Supreme Court. The Court reversed the conviction, holding that the right to motivation impeachment, a Sixth Amendment right, had been denied, citing *Davis v. Alaska*.

The United States Supreme Court took certiorari. They, in a not particularly decisive opinion, remanded the case back to the Delaware Supreme Court to determine if the denial of motivation impeachment may have been "harmless error."

Apparently the Delaware Supreme Court had seen enough of this case. The court found there was no "harmless error."

From these three opinions we distill the following:

1. It does not take much motivation to be impeachable.
2. Motivation impeachment is never collateral.
3. The "harmless error" rule may become an issue.

The "harmless error" rule deserves some comment. *Delaware v. Van Arsdale*, 475 U.S. 673 (1986) has put into play the possibility that the "harmless error" rule might be applied to motivation impeachment. The opinion has been cited as applying the "harmless error" rule to motivation impeachment.[27]

Obviously this conclusion may be somewhat questionable. *Van Arsdale* did not apply the "harmless error" rule in remanding the case. The Court merely suggested the Delaware Supreme Court consider whether it might apply in the case. The Delaware Supreme Court said it did not.

[27]*See Fuller v. Gorczyk*, 273 F.3d 212 (2d Cir. 2001) (holding a violation of the Sixth Amendment Confrontation Clause resulting from defendant's inability to cross-examine his wife concerning letters she wrote and statements she made referring to her lying about the charges and being intimidated by the prosecutor was harmless error where the letters had little independent probative value and the wife's testimony never wavered, and the defendant conceded that he did not think his wife invented the allegations against him); *United States v. Diaz*, 876 F.2d 1344, 1351 (7th Cir. 1989) (noting if the court had held the defendants were deprived of their Confrontation Clause rights, the deprivation would have been subject to the harmless error analysis established by *Van Arsdale*); *United States v. Chandler*, 326 F.3d 210 (3d Cir. 2003) (holding defendant's inability to exercise her Confrontation Clause rights that resulted from the prohibition of the defendant to cross-examine two government witnesses about their potential sentence reduction they believed they would earn for their testimony was an abuse of discretion and warranted reversal).

Against this history and background courts have, citing *Van Arsdale*, applied the "harmless error" rule to motivation impeachment.

When using motivation impeachment you are placing in question a witness's reliability and, it follows, credibility. You would be better served if you do not mention "credibility" to the trial judge. Some judges confuse motivation impeachment with truthfulness impeachment. The term "credibility" has contributed to this confusion.

Commendably, the Federal Rules of Evidence Committee addressed this issue by amending FRE 608(b). Effective in December 2003, the term "credibility" was deleted from the rule and "character trait for truthfulness" was substituted. This was an excellent change which should help lawyers and judges better understand and distinguish between both motivation and truthfulness impeachment.

How far can you go with motivation impeachment? Assume the all-too-common "felon in possession of a gun" federal case. What about "pushing the envelope" and crossing the arresting officer as follows:

Q: "Fair to say this is your case?"
Q: "You initiated it?"
Q: "You developed it?"
Q: "You have helped prosecute it?"
Q: "If Mr. Washington is convicted, you will receive some credit?"
Q: "On the other hand, if Mr. Washington is acquitted you will not look all that good?"
Q: "We can agree, it is important to you that Mr. Washington be convicted?"
Q: "You want him convicted?"
Q: "You would do most anything to get him convicted?"

The answer may well be "I would not." You will have made your point so move on.

Some judges might not allow this cross-examination, but then again some appellate courts might reverse as a denial of motivation impeachment, which it obviously is.

In any event, though its impact score would not be all that high, it would still be proper and helpful as motivation impeachment. The point we make is you should use imaginative ways to involve motivation impeachment.

We suggest a nonexhaustive list of situations where we might use motivation impeachment.

Several other motivation issues should be considered.

- **DEAL** – (this will be discussed further)
- **CRIMES** – (not just for snitch – issue is not what but when)
- **PENDING CHARGES** – (regardless of whether known to prosecutor or part of deal)
- **ARRESTS**
- **CRIMES – NO ARREST**
- **PROBATION**
- **POTENTIAL CHARGES OF FAMILY MEMBERS**
- **BENEFITS CONFERRED ON WITNESS BY PROSECUTOR**
- **COMFORTS OF LIVING** – housing arrangement, that is, extra visits, phone privileges, recreation time, programs, transportation to court, jobs, food
- **MONEY**
- **FAMILY BENEFITS** – housing, jobs
- **RELATIONSHIPS** – family: godmother, brother, sister, friends, roommates; ex-lover
- **EMPLOYER** – raises, promotions, personnel files
- **PREVIOUS RUN-INS** – disputes, quarrels
- **EXPERTS** – (1) dollarMoney in this case, work regularly for one side, stake in outcome, that is, future employment
- **GANG BIAS**
  - SAME GANG – rules, bylaws, pledges
  - OTHER GANG
  - EX–GANG MEMBER
- **MONEY**
- **RACE**
- **DECISION TO SPEAK TO BOTH SIDES – FOGELNEST** (This will be discussed later).

When you impeach with motivation impeachment, are you "opening the door" for redirect evidence? Unfortunately some trial courts erroneously believe this is so. In fact, where a witness has been impeached with motivation, "only when 'fairness' to the proponent of the witness dictates. . ." which seldom occurs, should an attempt to rehabilitate on redirect be allowed. See an excellent law review article by Professor Phillip W. Broadhead, a wonderful trial lawyer and former assistant public defender, in the *American Journal of Trial Advocacy*, Vol. 34:2, Fall 2010.

The DC Defender office won an interesting impeachment case in *Longus v. U.S.*, 52 A.3d 836 (2012). The trial court denied the defendant the right to use motivation impeachment in cross-examining a police officer's alleged witness coaching in a separate case.

The defense sought to impeach a police officer they had called as their witness. Obviously his testimony hurt more than it helped. Allowed to cross-examine him as a hostile witness also hurt more than it helped. The defense sought to impeach. They wanted to show he was being investigated for witness coaching in an unrelated case. The trial judge allowed the defense to bring out he was under investigation but would not allow them to go into the details.

This would obviously have been motivation impeachment, but interestingly the trial judge found it was "collateral." It is difficult to understand how this was "unimportant," and more to the point motivation impeachment, as we know is not subject to the "collateral" limitation.

The DC Circuit reversed properly finding there was a Sixth Amendment violation of the defendant's right to use motivation impeachment. Obviously, as the court noted, the witness would have had an incentive to carry favor with the prosecutor.

The impeachment could also have been on truthfulness. (The attorneys wisely choose to argue motivation.) The trial judge's mention of the "collateral" limitation could be understood if truthfulness were the issue.

Impeaching the Deal

Common sense tells us that impeaching the snitch, though it sounds good and indeed looks good to us as criminal defense attorneys, often has, unfortunately, a limited impact score. Whatever it is we throw at the snitch is often associated with our defendant. "Tell me who your friends are and I will tell you who you are." "Birds of a feather flock together." In defending the *Gotti* case the defense attorneys totally impeached and effectively destroyed the main prosecution witness. Still, the jury convicted.

Accepting this, criminal defense lawyers must be aware of the many avenues of potential "snitch" impeachment and, in particular, the potential for "bonus points." Bonus points come from facts which hurt the witness which you bring out in developing the impeachment.

Your rights to impeach on "the deal" are, as indeed they should be, extremely broad. They are limited not so much by "what" as by "when." To explain, a twenty-year-old uncharged felony could not be used, but a recent minor misdemeanor could. Strictly speaking there are no time limits as such, rather a common sense rule would apply.

So what are we talking about? What would be on our motivation impeachment of the snitch menu?

- Any and all bad acts if they are a crime, specifically including minor misdemeanors. Recall *Delaware v. Van Ardsale* where the bad act was public drunkenness. Does the witness either beat up his wife or kick the family dog when he comes home? *U.S. v. Hastings*, 577 F.2d 38, 40–41 (8th Cir. 1978).
- Uncharged crimes, again assuming they meet the common sense time limit criteria, may be used. As will be explained shortly, this would be so even if the prosecutor has no knowledge of these uncharged crimes. *U.S. v. Green*, 617 F.3d 233 (3d Cir. 2010).
- Arrests may be used. Again, the same reasonable time limit limitation applies and prosecutorial knowledge is not required.
- Obviously, as distilled from the above, crimes without arrests would be in play.

- The fact that the witness is on probation is obviously on the menu. This was the situation in *Davis v. Alaska*, 415 U.S. 308 (1974).
- Again, distilled from above, we know our menu is not restricted to things specifically included in the "deal." The test is not an objective one but rather a subjective one. That which a witness believes, his expectations, his hopes, and possibly even what he would like to happen are in play. The prosecutors' knowledge and actual promises do not limit our impeachment. *U.S. v. Turner*, 198 F.3d 425, 429–30 (4th Cir. 1999); *Giglio v. US*, 405 US 150, 154–55 (1972).

Motivation impeachment would obviously apply to the witness who was a paid informant, the witness who has denied talking to anybody about his testimony, the witness who was intensively coached, the witness who misrepresented his dealings with the police and the witness whose perjurious testimony was allowed to stand uncorrected by the prosecutor, and the witness who made a deal with the prosecutor after being threatened with spending the rest of his life in jail if he did not testify as to the prosecutors wanted him to.[28]

In *Banks* the prosecutor did not disclose any of this information, an obvious violation of *Brady v. Maryland*, 373 U.S. 83 (1963), which applies to exculpatory and impeaching material. The opinion cites *Lee v. U.S.*, 343 U.S. 747, 757 (1952) as to the "serious questions of credibility" posed by informants. The opinion also cites to the outstanding law review article authored by Judge Trott, "Words of Warning for Prosecutors Using Criminals as Witnesses," 47 Hastings L.J. 1381 (1996).

Surprisingly, indeed shockingly, the prosecutor argued to the Supreme Court that prosecutors "can lie and conceal" evidence.

The Robert Fogelnest "Truth Letter"

Related to motive impeachment is a letter Robert Fogelnest, an excellent and experienced criminal defense lawyer, often uses. The letter reads as follows:

September 17, 1999

[28] *See Banks v. Dretke*, 540 U.S. 668 (2004).

Re: United States v. Defendant

Mr./Ms. Rat
c/o Rat Lawyer
Address

Via First Class Mail and
Certified Mail/Return Receipt Requested

Dear Mr./Ms. Rat:

I represent [CLIENT] in regard to criminal charges which are pending against him in [LOCATION]. In order to properly represent [CLIENT], and to get all the facts before the jury so that they can determine the truth, it is important for me to investigate the case and to interview all of the witnesses. Because you have been identified as a witness I need to speak with you. My investigator and I are willing to meet with you under any arrangements that you want, at a time and place convenient to you. You may refuse to answer any questions asked and, of course, have your lawyer present during the interview. The purpose of this interview is not to embarrass you or to make you feel uncomfortable. My only purpose is to have you provide a completely truthful statement of all the facts and circumstances in this case.

Although the prosecutors can promise you many things, and even help you to avoid going to jail for the crimes which you have committed, I can't give you anything for speaking to us. However, since you have discussed this case with the prosecutor and other law enforcement agents, it seems fair that you speak with us as well so that we can determine the truth. Your attorney will confirm that witnesses do not belong to any one side. He or she will also confirm that it would be improper for the prosecutor or agents to prevent, or even suggest, that you not speak with us. It is solely your decision. It is, however, appropriate to discuss this request with your attorney, and I suggest that you do so.

Thank you for reading this letter. I hope that out of a sense of fairness and justice, you will do what is right. I believe that it is right for you to speak with us so that we may be better able to help the jury determine the truth. I hope that after consultation with your attorney you agree and decide to cooperate with us as you have with the prosecutors.

Yours truly,
Counsel for Defendant

Robert Fogelnest:
A typical impeachment based on motivation because a witness chooses only to speak to one side goes as follows:

Q: "We wanted and tried to speak to you?"
A: "Yes."
Q: "You refused?"
A: "Yes."

This line of questioning does not do justice to what a trial lawyer can and should do in this area. By using either a letter similar to the Fogelnest letter, or simply using similar language in an oral interview of a witness who likely will not speak to us, we can create something far greater and more effective.

Assume we intend to interview a witness knowing the witness (most likely due to motive, incidentally) will not speak with us. Before trial an investigation explains we would like to speak with you, Mr. Witness. "And we will do so at anytime and location convenient to you," to find out the truth." "Because we want to present the truth to a jury," "and because we believe it only fair that the witness speaks to both sides."

At a trial, rather than the two-line impeachment above, it goes like this:

Q: "On January 7, 2013, we came to see you?"
A: "Yes."
Q: "We introduced ourselves?"
A: "Yes."
Q: "We showed you identification?"
A: "Yes."

Q: "We told you we would speak with you at any time and location convenient to you?'

A: "Yes."

Q: "We told you we felt it fair that witnesses speak to both sides?"

A: "Yes."

Q: "We told you we wanted to present the *truth* to the jury?"

A: "Yes."

Q: "We asked you if you would tell us the *truth* about what happened?"

A: "Yes."

Q: "After asking you if you would tell us the truth about what happened, you choose not to speak to us?"

A: "Yes."

Through this line of questioning, which was set up by our pretrial investigation, we have impeached by motivation, demonstrating for the jury (who will always want the "truth"!), that at best, the witness is hiding something, and at worst, the witness is lying.

Bonus Point Potential

We learned from *U.S. v. Abel* the potential and powerful way to incorporate "bonus points." Now we will learn how to use and involve "bonus points" when impeaching as criminal defense lawyers, particularly in the federal courts on the deal.

Impeaching the Deal

The Setup

Q: "You do not like jail?" (plausibility cross)

A: "No."

Q: "You do not want to go back to jail?"

A: "No."[29]

---

[29]Many good and experienced criminal defense lawyers like and effectively use "a day in one's life in jail": you arise early in the morning; you march down to breakfast; the food is not all that good and there is not enough of it; you work all day – at a menial job; you are only paid two dollars an hour; the lunch and then the dinner is no better than the breakfast; you do not get time to spend with the few friends you have; you seldom are visited by your family; frequently there are outbreaks of violence; you are always in danger of being attacked and beaten up; you only get to go outside for one hour a day; when you are outside there is nothing to do; there are a lot of fights and much violence when you are outside; you

(continued)

Q: "You certainly do not want to go there for long?"
A: "No."
Q: "If you have to go back, the shorter the better?"
A: "Yes."
Q: "But the best would be if you do not have to go back to jail at all?"
A: "Yes."
Q: "That is what you would like to happen?"
A: "Yes."
Q: "You would do almost anything to avoid going back to jail?" (plausibility cross)
A: "Yes."
Q: "You would escape if you could?" (plausibility cross)
A: "Yes."
Q: "You would steal a car to avoid going back to jail?" (plausibility cross)
A: "Yes."
Q: "You would lie to avoid going back to jail?" (plausibility cross)[30]

His Problems

Q: "You know you committed crimes?"
A: "Yes."
Q: "You know the prosecutor can prove these crimes?"
A: "Yes."
Q: "That is why you are now in jail?"
A: "Yes."
Q: "Where you do not want to be?"
A: "Yes."

(footnote continued from previous page)
not like; you are actually scared your cell mate might hurt you; you do not have a TV; the bathroom in your cell is in the open; the lights go off at ten o'clock. (NOTE: a few of these might prove helpful, but using all or most of them would be "carrying coals to Newcastle.")

[30]Usually, not unlike seeking help on Who Wants to be a Millionaire by "phoning a friend," the witness will look at the prosecutor and hesitate before answering. Actually, the answer of the witness is not all that important. A "yes" answer will allow you to continue with "you would lie to help yourself." A "no" will, in the eyes of the jurors, brand the witness a liar.

Q: "You are concerned with how long you will have to spend in jail?"
A: "Yes."
Q: "How long the prosecutor can keep you there?"
A: "Yes."
Q: "You would like to know how long you will have to spend in jail?"
A: "Yes."
Q: "This is important to you?"
A: "Yes."

What He Does

Q: "You needed to talk to a lawyer to get these answers?"
A: "Yes."
Q: "So you did talk to a lawyer?"
A: "Yes."
Q: "He gave you some answers?"
A: "Yes."
Q: "He explained a little bit to you about the Federal Sentencing Guidelines?"
A: "Yes."
Q: "You asked him some questions?"
A: "Yes."
Q: "You learned something about the Federal Sentencing Guidelines?"
A: "Yes."
Q: "You were particularly interested in how long you could spend in jail?"
A: "Yes."
Q: "You wanted to know the maximum sentence you could receive?"
A: "Yes."
Q: "You certainly wanted to avoid that maximum sentence?"
A: "Yes."
Q: "You wanted to know how you could avoid that maximum sentence?"
A: "Yes."
Q: "You wanted to know who could help you avoid the maximum sentence?"
A: "Yes."

Do we have a problem with this line of questioning invading the attorney–client privilege? Not really.

1. The privilege belongs to the witness and only he can assert it. The prosecutor cannot claim it for him. In a word, the witness would have to claim the privilege in front of the jury. In effect he would be announcing he decided not to tell the truth and give us important information.
2. You can and should explain to the trial judge – if the witness seeks to claim the privilege – that you have no intention of going into the "actual conversation" between the witness and his attorney. You are simply inquiring about *what he knows*.
3. Finally, *Murdoch v. Castro*, 365 F.3d 699 (10th Cir. 2004) supports our inquiry.

The specific facts and assumptions in *Murdoch v. Castro* are not totally clear. Regardless, the opinion has great *dicta*.

Before the opening statements the prosecutor discovered a letter from her cooperating witness to the witness's attorney. The letter (1) disclaimed the witness's statement to the prosecutor, (2) allowed that the statement to the prosecutor was coerced, and (3) exonerated the defendant.

The cooperating witness's attorney, although apparently trying to help his client (one has to question his dedication and commitment to criminal defense work), asserted the attorney–client privilege.

Though it is difficult to understand how this was protected by the attorney–client privilege in that the prosecutor had a copy of the letter, the trial judge found it to be so.

The Tenth Circuit reversed and remanded. The letter contained inconsistent statement impeachment material. (It probably contained motivation impeachment material as well.) In effect, the court held that evidentiary privileges or laws must yield to a defendant's Sixth Amendment right to cross-examine. Such privileges and laws cannot bar access to evidence of inconsistent statements and ulterior motives of accomplices who serve as government witnesses.

Relationship and Investment with the Prosecutor

Q: "You knew there was only one way to avoid a long sentence?"
A: "Yes."
Q: "You knew there was only one person who could help you do this?"
A: "Yes."
Q: "That was the prosecutor?"
A: "Yes."
Q: "He was the only one who could help you on your sentence?"
A: "Yes."
Q: "You needed him as a friend?"
A: "Yes."
Q: "You needed him as someone who would help you?"
A: "Yes."
Q: "You needed him to help keep you out of jail?"
A: "Yes."
Q: "That is what was most important to you?"
A: "Yes."
Q: "To stay out of jail?"
A: "Yes."
Q: "You would do most anything to stay out of jail?"
A: "Yes."
Q: "So you decided to become his friend?"
A: "Yes."
Q: "You wanted him to be your friend?"
A: "Yes."
Q: "To do that you would have to do what he wanted?"
A: "Yes."
Q: "So you made a DEAL with him?"
A: "Yes."
Q: "A Deal to help yourself?"
A: "Yes."
Q: "A Deal to help you avoid a long sentence?"
A: "Yes."

The Deal Spelled out on a Chart[31]

Samples of two charts follow:

THE "DEAL"

Maximum sentence you will receive = 10 years
Hoping to do much better = Probation

OTHER CRIMES	POSSIBLE MAX. SENTENCE
• Crack Cocaine (5 grams or More) with Enhancement for Prior Felony Drug Conviction (WILL NOT CHARGE)	10 YEARS UP TO LIFE
• Failure to Pay Income Tax (5 Years) (WILL NOT CHARGE)	5 YEARS
• Probation Revocation (WILL NOT CHARGE)	5 YEARS
• ____Aggravated Assault (Domestic Violence) (WILL NOT CHARGE)	1 YEAR
• ____DWI (WILL NOT CHARGE)	1 YEAR
TOTAL	22 YEARS TO LIFE

THE DEAL = 22 YEARS TO LIFE vs. PROBATION

Start by showing the term "Deal" which you have taken from the witness: "I want to ask you some questions about your Deal with the prosecutor?"

Next spell out the specifics of the Deal, if there are specifics. "The maximum sentence you will receive is five years?" Then get into his subjective desires: what he would want, like, and hopes for.

[31]The chart should take the form most convenient to you. If you have Parker penmanship, a blackboard would be excellent. PowerPoint may work. Our preference, not having Parker penmanship and not being fans of PowerPoint, would be a demonstrative aid using Velcro.

DEAL

Expects: 12½ (max) – Probation (min)

Prosecutor will not charge:

• Crack Cocaine	3
• Felony Enhancement	20 (mandatory minimum)
• Income Tax	6
• Probation Revocation	5
Prosecutor made "go away":	
• Aggravated Assault	4
• DWI	1
39 Years vs. Probation	39 years

Q: "But you would hope to do even better than that five years?"
A: "Yes."
Q: "You would like to get probation?"
A: "Yes."
Q: "You know this might be possible?"
A: "Yes."
Q: "This would be what you want?"
A: "Yes."
Q: "This all depends on the prosecutor?"
A: "Yes."
Q: "Downward departures were explained to you?"
A: "Yes."
Q: "You know only the prosecutor can request a downward departure?"
A: "Yes."
Q: "You know only the prosecutor can recommend a downward departure?"
A: "Yes."
Q: "You want the prosecutor to recommend a downward departure?"
A: "Yes."
Q: "You want him on your side?"
A: "Yes."

Q: "You want him pleased with you?"
A: "Yes."
Q: "You would do most anything to please him?"
A: "Yes."
Q: "You would do most anything to make him happy?"
A: "Yes."

Now on the left hand side of your chart you start listing the crimes and bad things the witness has done. Obviously whatever they have on him would be a good start.

Across from the "crime or bad thing" list is the "possible maximum sentence." Always use the "possible *maximum* sentence."

In listing the "crimes and bad things" you must use your imagination. For instance, if he was selling dope he was making money. You know he did not report this money on his income tax returns, if indeed he even filed income tax returns.

Probation revocation is often in play.

Importantly, in that these things may have a high impact notwithstanding a low "possible maximum sentence" score, include his other minor criminal acts. Understand these other things need not have been charged. Did he beat up his wife or the family dog? Did he have a driving under the influence charge? All the better if the prosecutor, who actually need not know of these transgressions, "fixed" any of these cases.

Now add up his possible maximum sentence exposure. This should give you a good number, particularly when you contrast it with *his desire* for probation.

Conclusion

Q: "You do not want to go to jail?"
A: "Yes."
Q: "You would do most anything not to go to jail?"
A: "Yes."
Q: "You would much prefer a sentence of probation?"
A: "Yes."

Q: "All of this *depends* upon the Prosecutor?"
A: "Yes."
Q: "Whether or not he is satisfied with you?"
A: "Yes."
Q: "When you took the stand to tell your story, you did not know if the Prosecutor would be *satisfied* with you?"
A: "Yes."
Q: "You knew he would wait to make up his mind?"
A: "Yes."
Q: "He would wait to decide if he was satisfied?"
A: "Yes."
Q: "He would wait to decide if he would help you?"
A: "Yes."
Q: "You knew why he would wait?"
A: "Yes."
Q: "He did not trust you?"
A: "Yes."

Bonus Point Potential

Obviously "taking the sting out" of impeachment may not be a bad idea. You, in an effort to retain your "halo effect," will front and disclose the bad evidence.

A prosecutor might consider using Rule 607 to impeach her own "deal" with the witness on direct examination.

There are two arguments against this practice. First, you cannot claim the common law requirement of surprise. Then again, you are not calling this witness for the principal reason of bringing out the impeaching material.

Second, and probably more persuasively, the defense argument could be made that the prosecutor is seeking to "bolster" her witness before the witness has been attacked.

Whether a prosecutor can or cannot impeach their "deal" witness, their attempt to be the first to disclose this information should not be successful. The defense can, and indeed should, expose the "deal" in opening statement.

CHAPTER 4

Truthfulness

This method of impeachment is spelled out in FRE 608. Rule 608 reads as follows:

> **Rule 608.** A Witness's Character for Truthfulness or Untruthfulness.
>
> (a) **Reputation or Opinion Evidence.** A witness's credibility may be attacked or supported by testimony about the witness's reputation for having a character for truthfulness or untruthfulness, or by testimony in the form of an opinion about that character. But evidence of truthful character is admissible only after the witness's character for truthfulness has been attacked.
>
> (b) **Specific Instances of Conduct.** Except for a criminal conviction under Rule 609, extrinsic evidence is not admissible to prove specific instances of a witness's conduct in order to attack or support the witness's character for truthfulness. But the court may, on cross-examination, allow them to be inquired into if they are probative of the character for truthfulness or untruthfulness of: (**1**) the witness; or (**2**) another witness whose character the witness being cross-examined has testified about.
>
> By testifying on another matter, a witness does not waive any privilege against self-incrimination for testimony that relates only to the witness's character for truthfulness.

For the most part, this rule is often misunderstood, underappreciated, and usually not sufficiently or well used as a method of impeachment.

We list it number four on our list of ways to impeach. Its frequency of use score is a six and one-half. It has an impact score around eight. It does have evidentiary limitations that limit its score.

Every witness who testifies puts their character trait for truthfulness in issue. This truthfulness trait may be impeached in two distinct ways.

The least common, indeed the seldom used way, is through the use, on direct examination, of negative character witness. This will be covered at the end of this chapter.

Far more commonly, the witness's truthfulness is impeached during the cross-examination of the witness. This we now cover.

When we speak of truthfulness we are usually (though as later explained we are not always so limited) talking about "lies" – basic mendacity.

The lie must be specific. One cannot ask (which, in any event, being a "question" and not a statement should not be done on cross-examination) a witness if he or she ever lied.

Also, there must be a "good faith" basis to justify the truthfulness cross-examination (*U.S. v. Davis*, 609 F.3d 663 (5th Cir. 2010); *U.S. v. Katsougrakis*, 715 F.2d 769 (2d Cir. 1983)).

That said the limitations, except for the legal evidentiary one, are basically to be found in common sense. Though there are no time[33] or substance limits on the lies that may be used, common sense should give us limits. For instance, assuming some fifteen years ago the witness lied to his second-grade teacher as to why he was absent from school, you could use this lie but you would be stupid to do so.[34]

Investigative sources to discover lies are extensive: job applications, applications for loans, leases, or whatever things said at depositions or in court, particularly at sentencing hearings. Former spouses or former business associates (particularly assuming the business failed) are great sources.

[33]The drafters of the rules had included a time limit but the Congress eliminated it.
[34]See, however, when we talk about "negative character witnesses," how this might be effectively used.

Actually, as mentioned above, truthfulness impeachment is not limited to lies. *U.S. v. Mansky*, 186 F.3d 770 (7th Cir. 1999). *Mansky* is an interesting opinion written by Judge Flaum. The opinion adopts a "middle view" of the arguments made by the prosecutor and the defense as to the proper scope of Rule 608(b). It includes within the scope of the rule behavior seeking personal advantage by taking from others in violation of their rights; theft, stealing, buying, receiving or using stolen property; bribery; deceptive practice; failure to file income tax returns; and finally the facts in the case, threats to witnesses in an earlier case.

Also, *Mansky* comments on the Ninth Circuit case of *U.S. v. Foster*, 227 F.3d 1096, 1100 (9th Cir. 2000), which suggests lawyers do not fully understand the rule.

In that this book is about all of the ways to impeach, a comment on *U.S. v. Mansky*, 186 F.3d 770 (7th Cir. 1999) seems appropriate. The impeachment attempt sought to use Rule 608 – truthfulness. The trial court's denial of the impeachment led to a wonderful Rule 608 opinion in the Seventh Circuit. This should be, but is not, the end of the story.

The same impeachment predicated upon physical threats to witnesses in an earlier federal case could easily and appropriately have been introduced as motivation impeachment. Obviously it involved a federal crime. The witness had made a "deal" with the prosecutor. It could have been included on your "DEAL" chart as a crime. The advantage to upgrading to motivation impeachment would have been you could and would have avoided possible problems with the "collateral" limitation.

On the other hand, we might not now have the wonderful and helpful *Mansky* opinion.

Unfortunately, truthfulness impeachment has a major limitation, one that to us makes little or no sense. You obviously know where we are coming from.

We have learned that some inconsistent statement impeachment is collateral and some is noncollateral. We have also learned that motivation impeachment is never collateral. Now we learn (and we wonder why impeachment is so confusing) that *all truthfulness impeachment is collateral.*

Rule 608(b) specifically tells us that specific instances of untruthfulness may not be proved by extrinsic evidence.[35, 36]

There is not much you can do with this "collateral" limitation. First, you confront the witness with a lie. However, if the witness lies a second time and denies the first lie, he does so with impunity. Obviously two lies are better than one!

There are three things you can and should do when you anticipate or are confronted with a denial, the second lie. First, aware that you must have a "basis in fact," you announce to the judge, with the jury present, that you intend to use 608 impeachment to show the witness is a liar. In support of this proposed impeachment you give the court and the prosecutor your "basis in fact," a copy of a job application. Not bad. At the least, the judge will see the second lie and the jury knows the prosecutor has a copy of the document. Also, the witness knows the judge has a copy of the document. This production alone may convince the witness to answer *truthfully and acknowledge* the lie.

Second, anticipation of the second lie, you can use what we call the "persuasive document." To explain: you have a job application submitted by the witness. As with most job applications, it included the question "Have you ever been convicted of a crime?" Our witness lied on the application and answered the question "no." Knowing his propensity to lie, you are both fearful and correct in assuming he will again lie and deny you the opportunity to perfect your truthfulness impeachment.

Use the "persuasive document." Obviously, the job application, which you have presented to the judge and the prosecutor, will serve as the "persuasive document." Make an obvious point of holding and reading from the job application while you conduct this portion of your cross-examination. (No, you cannot and will not show or flash it to the jury. But if done correctly, you should achieve the same result.)

Not only will you hold the job application but more importantly you will obviously turn the pages and conspicuously read from the "persuasive document." (Something you would not otherwise want to or be required

[35]"[E]xtrinsic evidence is not admissible to prove specific instances of a witness's conduct in order to attack or support the witness's character for truthfulness." *Fed. R. Evid.* 608.
[36]*See United States v. Green*, 258 F.3d 683, 692 (7th Cir. 2001)

to do.) Importantly, make sure the jury can see you are reading from the job application.

With little practice you can master this technique. *Holding the document in your hands and reading from it* during your truthfulness impeachment, it will go as follows:

Q: "I want to ask you some questions about the job application you signed on September 6th of this year?" (conspicuously turning the pages to read from the last page.)
A: "Yes."
Q: "You signed (reading) the name John Smith?"
A: "Yes."
Q: "That was on page (reading) five?"
A: "Yes."
Q: "You dated it?"
A: "Yes."
Q: "(reading) September 6, 2011?"
A: "Yes."

(Make it obvious you are going back to the first page.)

Q: "(reading) That was with the XYZ Corporation?"
A: "Yes."
Q: "(reading) At 1510 West Diversey?"
A: "Yes."
Q: "(reading) In Chicago, Illinois?"
A: "Yes."
Q: "That job application had six pages?" (thumbing through them)
A: "Yes."
Q: "There were forty-seven questions?" (looking at the last page)
A: "Yes."
Q: "I want to ask you about question twenty-two."
A: "Yes."
Q: "That was on page four?" (thumbing through)
A: "Yes."

Q: "That question reads (and you read), 'Have you ever been convicted of a crime?'"

A: "Yes."

Q: "You answered that question?"

A: "Yes."

Q: "(reading) You answered that question 'no'?"

A: "Yes."

If the witness answers honestly, you may proceed to develop and expound on the lie. However, if the witness lies again you show total surprise and disgust.[37]

Q: "You are, under oath, telling this jury you answered question twenty-two 'yes'?"

A: "Yes."

Q: "Would you like to read your answer?" (The form, a question, is terrible and may well be objected to. A good try, but it is improper.)

- "Your honor, may I show the jury his answer to question twenty-two?"
- Prosecutor: "Objection." (Might this be suborning perjury?)
- Judge: "Sustained." (The correct ruling.)

This is about the best that you can do. The jury knows you are "reading" from the job application and hopefully your credibility is such that they know you would not misread the document, a document you were trying to show them.

By objecting, though legally proper, the prosecutor is protecting the witness from being shown to be a liar. This will not be lost on the jury.

---

[37]There is another possibility. The witness may answer that he "does not know" or "does not remember." For you this is not a bad answer. In effect, the witness has invited you to "refresh his recollection." You are now allowed to show the witness the job application. Showing the witness the answer on the job application should shame and possibly even scare him into admitting the lie. If it does not, you are back where you started, faced with the "collateral" limitation, except that the jury knows you showed the witness the job application.

There is still a third thing you might want to do. Professor Charles Rose, who heads up the outstanding trial advocacy program at the Stetson University College of Law, shared this with us.

Knowing him to be one of the best and imaginative teachers of trial advocacy, we listened and now include his suggestion.

As soon as the witness lies, you should request that the trial judge (who, recall, has a copy of the job application) allow the witness to consult with counsel as he may be walking into or inviting a perjury charge. In truth, the probability of this is for the most part nonexistent. Prosecutors seldom, if indeed ever, indict their own witnesses for perjury, particularly where the perjury was intended to help the prosecutor.

Develop the Lies

Lies are not always all that impactful. We must do something more with them. There is not a lot we can do but we can, and should, give them additional impact or meaning. In a word, we should "milk them a bit."

Where the witness admits to the lie, you follow up your cross-examination as follows:

Q: "You were not being accurate?"
A: "Yes."
Q: "You did not tell the truth?"
A: "Yes."
Q: "You lied?"
A: "Yes."
Q: "You lied for a reason?" (Everybody lies for a reason.)
A: "Yes."
Q: "You lied to help yourself?" (Everybody lies to help themself.)
A: "Yes."

Did the Witness Use an Alias?

This circumstance would be far more prevalent in criminal cases. Whatever, the point to be made is that the use of an alias is a lie. Unfortunately, unless you have something to work with and know how to use truthfulness impeachment on the alias, it will have little, if any, impact.

To start with, many people with whom we are familiar use aliases. Most obviously movie stars use aliases. Again, facts permitting, you have to "milk it" and even get in a few "bonus points."

The facts will particularly help you if, most probably in a criminal case, the witness has a sheet of convictions or even merely arrests.

Q: "I want to ask you some questions about your name, you understand?"
A: "Yes."
Q: "Your name is Dale Cobb?"
A: "Yes."
Q: "That is your only real name?"
A: "Yes."
Q: "That is your only official name?"
A: "Yes."
Q: "That is the name your father and mother gave you when you were born?"
A: "Yes."
Q: "You have never legally changed your name?"
A: "No."
Q: "Your only legal name is Dale Cobb?"
A: "Yes."
Q: "I want to ask you some questions about your arrest[38] back in January of 2000, you understand?"
A: "Yes."
Q: "That was for armed robbery?"
A: "Yes."
Q: "You were taken to the police station?"
A: "Yes."
Q: "The police asked you questions?"
A: "Yes."
Q: "They asked you your name?"
A: "Yes."

[38]If this draws an objection, explain to the judge that you are not impeaching under Rule 609, but rather you will be using Rule 608 Truthfulness Impeachment. The fact of the arrest, even without the necessity of a conviction, will give you "bonus points."

Q: "You told them your name was Don Clark?"
A: "Yes."

Develop the Lie

Q: "That was not accurate?"
A: "No."
Q: "You did not tell the truth?"
A: "No."
Q: "Your name was not Don Clark?"
A: "No."
Q: "Your name was Dale Cobb?"
A: "Yes."
Q: "You lied to the police?"
A: "Yes."
Q: "You knew you were lying?"
A: "Yes."
Q: "It did not bother you to lie?"
A: "No."
Q: "You lied for a reason?"
A: "Yes."
Q: "To escape criminal punishment?"
A: "Yes."
Q: "You lied to help yourself?"
A: "Yes."
Q: "You did not want them to know who you really were?"
A: "Yes."
Q: "You had a good reason to not want them to know who you really were?"
A: "Yes."
Q: "If they knew who you really were, they would know you were a convicted felon?"
A: "Yes."
Q: "You did not want them to know you were a convicted felon?"
A: "Yes."

Keep Going

Q: "I now want to ask you some questions about your arrest in February of 2002. You understand?"
A: "Yes."
Q: "That was for indecent liberties with a minor?"
A: "Yes."
Q: "Again, you were taken to the police station?"
A: "Yes."
Q: "Again, the police asked you your name?"
A: "Yes."
Q: "You told them your name was Dale Clark?"
A: "Yes."

Develop the Lie

Q: "But that was not accurate?"
A: "No."
Q: "You did not tell the police the truth?"
A: "No."
Q: "Your name was not Dale Clark?"
A: "No."
Q: "Your name was Dale Cobb?"
A: "Yes."
Q: "Once again you lied to the police?"
A: "Yes."
Q: "Once again you lied for a reason?"
A: "Yes."
Q: "Once again, you lied to help yourself?"
A: "Yes."
Q: "You did not want them to know who you really were?"
A: "Yes."
Q: "Again, you had a good reason to not want the police to know who you really were?"
A: "Yes."

Q: "If the police knew who you really were, they would know you were a convicted felon?"
A: "Yes."
Q: "Again, you did not want them to know you were a convicted felon?"
A: "Yes."
Q: "So you again lied to the police to help and protect yourself?"
A: "Yes."

A Side Issue

The courts may well be creating an unnecessary truthfulness issue. Where an earlier trial judge has, in a totally unrelated case, found a police officer testified falsely, should a defendant be able to impeach the officer with truthfulness? Why not, for whatever good it will do.

But this was not the ruling of the Second Circuit in *U.S. v. Cedeno*, 644 F.3d 79 (2d Cir. 2011). The trial court would not allow the impeachment and the Second Circuit affirmed.

Obviously the defense attorney could not try to impeach by asking the witness (again, as a matter of style we should "tell" the witness and not "ask" him) if another judge had found he had falsified his testimony. This approach would have improperly used "extrinsic evidence" (the opinion of the judge).

Conceding that, the defense attorney should have been able to impeach with "you lied when you testified in the such-and-such case?"

The obvious answer would be "no," and that would be the end of this issue.

Our own Seventh Circuit has addressed this issue, if not particularly well. The opinion is in response to a rehearing request by the prosecutor. The conviction was affirmed, but the prosecutor took issue with certain language in the opinion. *U.S. v. Dawson and Ingram*, 434 F.3d 956 (7th Cir. 2006).

First, the court said the trial judge had "discretion" to allow the defense to cross, and more specifically, to impeach three government agents on whether they had lied in two earlier suppression hearings. Obviously this would have been classic truthfulness impeachment. Why does, or should, the trial judge have "discretion?"

The trial judge would not allow the impeachment but the Seventh Circuit still affirmed the conviction.

Second, this was the reason the prosecutors sought rehearing. The Seventh Circuit extended the trial court's "discretion" to allowing the impeachment to include a reference to the fact that other judges had found the witnesses not to be credible.

The prosecutor had a good point. What other judges had found would have included the type of extrinsic evidence proscribed by Rule 608(b).

The court's opinion cites but obviously does not follow Professor Stephen A. Saltzburg's comment in "Impeaching the Witness: Prior Bad Acts and Extrinsic Evidence," 7 *Crim. Just.* 28, 31 (Winter 1995): ". . . counsel should not be permitted to circumvent the no-extrinsic-evidence provision by tucking a third person's opinion about prior acts into a question asked of a witness who has denied the act." As usual, the professor is "on the money."

Negative Character Witnesses

This is the mystery subject. Very few trial lawyers know of the existence of negative character evidence, and even fewer trial lawyers have ever used it. This is in part due to our unfamiliarity with character evidence in general.

Repeating what we said earlier, every witness who testifies puts their character for truthfulness in issue. Obviously when we think of truthfulness we think of lies, and we think of impeaching the lies during cross-examination. This is not bad thinking as this is the way truthfulness impeachment usually works. Now we will suggest a totally different, albeit seldom seen, way of using truthfulness impeachment to impeach under FRE 608.

For the most part, when we think of impeachment we think of cross-examination. With the exception of contradiction impeachment we usually impeach with cross-examination. Now, for want of some variety, we are going to impeach using direct examination. We are going to impeach with Rule 608 negative character witnesses, witnesses we will put on the stand, and direct examine in our case in chief.

To do this we need to familiarize ourselves with the somewhat convoluted and at times confusing use of character evidence.

Briefly stated, there are three ways to present character testimony. Two are permissible, the third is not.

In obedience to our common law heritage, we can prove a character trait (under FRE 608 the only one we can use is truthfulness) by establishing the untruthful reputation of the witness we are impeaching. This was the only way it could be done at common law, and it remains one of the ways we can do it today.

In truth, we are less proving a character trait for untruthfulness as we are developing the community "gossip." Accepting this, it remains one of the ways to prove the character trait for untruthfulness.

Wisely, the drafters of the Federal Rules of Evidence concluded that most character witnesses were simply testifying to their "opinion" rather than the "local gossip" or supposed reputation of the witness. Accepting this, they gave us a second way to prove character. The witness could give their "opinion" of the truthfulness (or apart from FRE 608) whatever the pertinent trait might be.

The third possible way of proving character, "specific instances of conduct," which for the most part would be, when using Rule 608, specific lies, cannot be gone into when using a character witness. Though understandable, this is interesting in that when we cross-examine with truthfulness tmpeachment we do use "specific instances" or specific lies.

If you are not now a bit confused, give yourself an "A." Parenthetically, it is not surprising that negative character witness is seldom used. Still, if you are willing to give it a try it can be a powerful weapon and an excellent way to impeach a witness.

We will do it. We will call a few "negative character" witnesses.

Q: "Mr. O'Brien why are you here today?" (This sets up primacy.)

A: "I have known A.J. Kramer for over 30 years, I think I know him better than anybody, including his three wives. I want to tell this court what a terrible liar he is."

Q: "Would you introduce yourself to the jury?" (Never use the "stupid" state your full name for the record and spell your last name for the court reporter.)

A: ". . ."

Q: "(Now use a few questions to make the witness more likeable and possibly to help the jury identify with him.)"

A: ". . ."

Q: "How long have you known Mr. Kramer?"

A: "More than 30 years."

Q: "How do you know him?"

A: ". . ."

Q: "Do you know other people who know him?" (Required to prove "reputation.")

A: ". . ."

Q: "Have you ever talked to these other people about his reputation for truthfulness?"

A: ". . ."

Q: "Would you tell the jury what his reputation for truthfulness is?"

A: "He is the biggest and worst liar any of us know."

Now Personal Opinion

Q: "You have told us you know Mr. Kramer for more than 30 years. During that time have you had many dealings with him?"

A: "Yes."

Q: "Based upon the long time you have known him and the many dealings you have had with him, do you have a personal opinion as to his honesty and truthfulness?"

A: "Yes."

Q: "Would you share with the jury your opinion as to his honesty and truthfulness?"

A: "He is the biggest liar I have ever known."

Q: "If he, like you have, were to take an oath on a bible to tell the truth, would you believe him?[39]

A: "No. He could take his oath on five bibles and I still would not believe him."

---

[39]*U.S. v. Bambulas*, 471 F.2d 501, 504 (7th Cir. 1972); *U.S. v. Walka*, 313 F.2d 236 (10th Cir. 1936).

A Final Test on Truthfulness

The defendant in a federal criminal case takes the stand. He had been convicted of "receiving stolen property," a misdemeanor. The prosecutor impeaches him with the misdemeanor under FRE 609, which is covered in the next chapter.

The defendant is convicted and appeals, arguing the "receiving stolen property" misdemeanor was not a crime involving "dishonesty or false statement," and accordingly should not have been used to impeach. For reasons explained in the next chapter the argument is well made and the Ninth Circuit agreed. See *United States v. Foster*, 227 F.3d 1096, 1100 (9th Cir. 2000). The conviction is reversed and remanded.

What does this have to do with us, and in particular truthfulness impeachment? Had the prosecutor read this chapter he would have known of *United States v. Mansky* and could and would have impeached using 608 Truthfulness rather than 609.

CHAPTER 5
Convictions

Rule 609. Impeachment by Evidence of a Criminal Conviction.

(a) **In General.** The following rules apply to attacking a witness's character for truthfulness by evidence of a criminal conviction: (**1**) for a crime that, in the convicting jurisdiction, was punishable by death or by imprisonment for more than one year, the evidence: (**A**) must be admitted, subject to Rule 403, in a civil case or in a criminal case in which the witness is not a defendant; and (**B**) must be admitted in a criminal case in which the witness is a defendant, if the probative value of the evidence outweighs its prejudicial effect to that defendant; and (**2**) for any crime regardless of the punishment, the evidence must be admitted if the court can readily determine that establishing the elements of the crime required proving – or the witness's admitting – a dishonest act or false statement.

(**b**) **Limit on Using the Evidence after 10 Years.** This subdivision (b) applies if more than 10 years have passed since the witness's conviction or release from confinement for it, whichever is later. Evidence of the conviction is admissible only if: (**1**) its probative value, supported by specific facts and circumstances, substantially outweighs its prejudicial effect; and (**2**) the proponent gives an adverse party reasonable written notice of the intent to use it so that the party has a fair opportunity to contest its use.

(c) **Effect of a Pardon, Annulment, or Certificate of Rehabilitation.** Evidence of a conviction is not admissible if: (1) the conviction has been the subject of a pardon, annulment, certificate of rehabilitation, or other equivalent procedure based on a finding that the person has been rehabilitated, and the person has not been convicted of a later crime punishable by death or by imprisonment for more than one year; or (2) the conviction has been the subject of a pardon, annulment, or other equivalent procedure based on a finding of innocence.

(d) **Juvenile Adjudications.** Evidence of a juvenile adjudication is admissible under this rule only if: (1) it is offered in a criminal case; (2) the adjudication was of a witness other than the defendant; (3) an adult's conviction for that offense would be admissible to attack the adult's credibility; and (4) admitting the evidence is necessary to fairly determine guilt or innocence.

(e) **Pendency of an Appeal.** A conviction that satisfies this rule is admissible even if an appeal is pending. Evidence of the pendency is also admissible.

Impeachment with convictions presented no problems in early common law England. Those convicted were summarily executed and therefore would never appear as witnesses.

England, in effect, went from one extreme to the other. In making a change they initially stopped off (midway) and allowed convicted felons to be impeached. For some time now, to the surprise of most American lawyers, England has not and does not allow convicted felons to be impeached with their convictions.

But, with the commendable exception of Hawaii,[39] we have, since 1917, when the Supreme Court put an end to the practice of excluding, on competency grounds, the testimony of those convicted of a crime, allowed

---

[39]Both by decision, *Hawaii v. Santiago*, 492 F. 2d 657 (1971), and by rule, Hawaii Rules of Evidence, Chapter 626, Rule 609, the right to impeach with a conviction, particularly impeaching a criminal defendant, is severely limited.

defendants to be impeached with those crimes. *Rosen v. U.S.* 245 U.S. 467, 471 (1917).

This background is helpful to our understanding the history of FRE 609 and how we arrived where we are today.

We adopted the midway point in English common law, by allowing convicted felons to be impeached with their convictions. The wisdom of this decision can be questioned.

We are told that impeachment goes to credibility. It is totally conceivable that a convicted murderer, a draft resister, or even a drug dealer or user, might be totally credible. Yet their convictions invite their impeachment, the strong impact of which has much to do with their being bad persons, and little or nothing to do with their credibility.

Against this historical background an otherwise-run-of-the-mill case was argued in the DC Circuit. *Luck v. U.S.*, 348 F.2d 763 (D.C. Cir. 1965). The fact that the defendant was impeached with a conviction was, with little chance of success, argued to the court.

As faith would have it, several Justices from the High Court in England were visiting our country. They were guests of the DC Court of Appeals and as such were invited to sit with the Court of Appeals during the day's oral arguments, and have dinner with them that evening.

Judge J. Skelly Wright, a giant of a man and a great jurist, personally related to senior MacCarthy this story. He sat with his DC Circuit and the visiting English Justices.

During the dinner the judges obviously talked about the cases that had been argued that morning. Save for one of several issues in the *Luck* case, there was little discussion or interest in the case. On one issue, the English Justices expressed surprise, indeed total shock, that we would, under any circumstances, allow a convicted felon to be impeached with his conviction. The defendant's case, they explained, would obviously be irreparably destroyed by allowing reference to the earlier conviction. They suggested that under no circumstance could this be fair.

Their concern and arguments were not lost on the DC Court of Appeals Judges, at least two of them. So it was the *Luck* opinion, expressing concern for the all too obvious prejudice a criminal defendant would suffer were an earlier conviction made known to the jury, made a major change in the law.

Judge McGowan, who authored the opinion, in an effort to ameliorate the problem, gave us a "balancing test" – a requirement that we weigh prejudice vs. probative value before allowing conviction impeachment of a criminal defendant.[40] Judge Wright agreed with Judge McGowan and Judge Danaher dissented.

No other Circuit followed or adopted *Luck*, but commendably the drafters of the Federal Rules of Evidence did adopt a "balancing test," albeit a different one. Actually, the "balancing test" in Rule 609 is better than the *Luck* test.

Against that background we now have FRE 609. The rule suggests many evidentiary issues, issues for the most part left to books on evidence. We discuss Rule 609 in the somewhat limited sense of its general applicability to trial lawyers as a method of impeachment.

Subject to certain later-discussed limitations, you, be it a civil or criminal case, may impeach if the witness's conviction was either a "*FELONY*" or involved "*DISHONESTY*" or "*FALSE STATEMENT.*"

If you have a felony and it does not involve "dishonesty or false statement," a "balancing test" limitation applies.

As the language suggests, there are actually two different balancing tests. One applies only to defendants in criminal cases. This is spelled out in Rule 609.[41] The other balancing test applies to all other witnesses. This second balancing test is spelled out in Rule 403.[42]

Obviously the two balancing tests are intended to make it more difficult to impeach, in particular a criminal defendant, with a conviction. This is as it should be, though again the argument could be made that only convictions involving "dishonesty and false statements" should and could be used against any witness.

---

[40]See an excellent law review article arguing that impeachment of a criminal defendant with a conviction should not be allowed. "Between Rock and a Hard Place: The Right to Testify and Impeachment by Prior Conviction," Alan D. Hornstein, 42 *Villanova Law Rev.* 1 (1997).
[41]See an excellent article by Stuart Green: "Deceit and Classification of Crimes: Federal Rule of Evidence 609(a)(2) and the Origins of Crimen Falsi," 99 *The Journal of Criminal Law and Criminology* 5087 (2000).
[42]Rule 403. Excluding Relevant Evidence for Prejudice, Confusion, Waste of Time, or Other Reasons. The court may exclude relevant evidence if its probative value is substantially outweighed by a danger of one or more of the following: unfair prejudice, confusing the issues, misleading the jury, undue delay, wasting time, or needlessly presenting cumulative evidence.

How Should the Courts "Balance?"

Looking first at the easier of the "balancing tests," Rule 403's "substantially outweighed" by the danger of prejudice test, we find few problems. Actually, there were problems with Rule 609 as initially written. In mentioning the "balancing test" it was only applied if the prejudice was "against the defendant." Did this exclude civil plaintiffs but give some protection to civil defendants? Obviously, this would not have been the intention of the drafters.

Though an interesting issue, it is one we need no longer concern ourselves with. The issue was brought home when the United States Supreme Court correctly, though with less-than-favorable and fair results, decided *Green v. Bock Laundry Machine Co.*, 490 U.S. 504 (1989). The trial court, again interpreting the rule as initially drafted, allowed a civil defendant to impeach the plaintiff with a conviction. To those familiar with the case this impeachment (the impact is always substantial) resulted in a judgment for the defendant.

Commendably, the Federal Rules of Evidence Committee, amended the rule in 1990 by specifically incorporating the Rule 403 "balancing test" to all witnesses other than criminal defendants.

In amending Rule 609 so as to incorporate the Rule 403 "balancing" test the Rules Committee gave prosecutors and criminal defense lawyers helpful guidance, guidance which in all probability should apply to civil trial lawyers. Specifically the committee noted,

> The second change effected by the amendment resolves an ambiguity as to the relationship of Rules 609 and 403 with respect to impeachment of witnesses other than the criminal defendant. . . The amendment applies the general balancing test of Rule 403 to protect all litigants against unfair impeachment of witnesses. The balancing test protects civil litigants, the government in criminal cases, and the defendant in a criminal case who calls other witnesses.[43]

---

[43]Fed. R. Evid. 609 advisory committee's notes (1990 Amendment).

"Balancing" where a criminal defendant is the witness does create some confusion and problems.[44]

Several well-reasoned cases list circumstances that would acerbate prejudice against a criminal defendant.[45]

What Amounts to Dishonesty or False Statement?

Where "dishonesty or false statement" exists, the impeaching lawyer has much more to work with. To start with, the "balancing" test does not apply. Also, the conviction need not be a felony.

You can impeach with a misdemeanor conviction.

That said, the courts usually, and most properly, interpret these terms of "dishonesty and false statement" narrowly. (This is in contrast, though understandably, with the way the courts interpret "untruthfulness" when considering truthfulness impeachment.)[46] The case law supports this conclusion.

Congress has "narrowly defined" the "crimen falsi" offenses of "dishonesty and false statement" contemplated by Rule 609(a)(2). *U.S. v. Belt*, 169 U.S. App. D.C. 1, 9, 514 F.2d 837, 845 (1975, *en banc*); *U.S. v. Millines*, 535 F.2d 121 (CT App. D.C. 1976).

Also the congressional debate on Rule 609 is instructive. The Report of the House and Senate Conference Committee tells us

> [b]y the phrase "dishonesty and false statement" the Conference means crimes such as perjury or subornation of perjury, false statement, criminal fraud, bezzlement, or false pretense, or any other offense in the nature of crimen falsi, the commission of which involves some element of deceit, untruthfulness, or falsification bearing on the accused's propensity to testify truthfully.[47]

It would – and does follow then – that where the conviction has a necessary element of proof involving one of the deceitful elements mentioned

[44] *United States v. Mahone*, 537 F.2d 922 (7th Cir. 1976).
[45] *See U.S. v. Givens*, 767 F.2d 574 (9th Cir.), cert, denied, 474 U.S. 953 (1985)
[46] *See United States v. Mansky*, 186 F.3d 770 (7th Cir. 1999).
[47] Fed. R. Evid. 609 advisory committee's notes (1974 Enactment Note to Subdivision (a)).

above; it would be considered as one involving "dishonesty or false statement."[48]

There are several related issues, issues best left to the learned discussions of the evidence teachers and their excellent books.

We do suggest a reading of an excellent en banc opinion from the Ninth Circuit, *United States v. Brackeen*, 969 F.2d 827 (9th Cir. 1992). The defendant, being tried for aiding and abetting an armed bank robbery, was impeached with two unarmed bank robbery convictions. The trial court found these crimes to have involved "dishonesty or false statement" and accordingly to be admissible without the need of a "balancing" test.

The Ninth Circuit reversed the conviction, specifically holding that ". . . Congress intended Rule 609(a)(2) to apply only to those crimes that factually or by definition entail some *element* of misrepresentation or deceit, and not to those crimes which, bad though they are, do not carry with them a tinge of falsification."

There remains a final and usually confusing issue. What if the crime itself does not require proof of dishonesty or false statement, but misrepresentation or deceit were involved in the commission of the crime?

A majority of the Circuits would allow the trial judge to use the underlying facts of the case to justify Rule 609(a)(2) impeachment. This reasoning may not make a great deal of sense.[49]

Remoteness

Rule 609 places a time limit on impeachable crimes. The time limit is ten years – ten years from the date of the conviction or the release from the

---

[48] *See U.S. v. Cameron*, 814 F.2d 403, 407 (7th Cir. 1987).

[49] "The '[o]verwhelmingly. . . practice is to allow and even encourage inquiry into underlying facts.'" Stuart P. Green, *Deceit and the Classification of Crimes: Federal Rule of Evidence 609(a)(2) and the Origins of Crimen Falsi*, 90 J. Crim. L. & Criminology 1087, 1120 (2000) (quoting 3 Christoper B. Mueller & Laird C. Kirkpatrick, *Federal Evidence*, § 278, at 270 (2d ed. 1994)); *see also United States v. Mejia-Alarcon*, 995 F.2d 982, 989–90 (10th Cir. 1993), cert. denied, 114 S.Ct. 334 (1994); *Altobello v. Borden Confectionary Products, Inc.*, 872 F.2d 215, 216 (7th Cir. 1989); *United States v. Givens*, 767 F.2d 574, 579 n.1 (9th Cir. 1985); *United States v. Lipscomb*, 702 F.2d 1049 (D.C. Cir. 1983); and *United States v. Grandmont*, 680 F.2d 867, 870–72 (1st Cir. 1982); *but cf. United States v. Lewis*, 626 F.2d 940, 946 (D.C. Cir. 1980).

conviction's confinement, whichever is the later date. Confinement would include probation or parole.

This limitation can be avoided if

- You give sufficient advance written notice to your adversary that you intend to use this impeachment so as to allow them to contest or object to the impeachment; and
- ". . . the court determines, in the interest of justice, that the probative value of the conviction supported by specific facts and circumstances substantially outweighs its prejudicial effect." (FRE 609(b)).

It would seem waving the "remoteness" limitation would favor a criminal defendant – they, more than most other witnesses, would be exposed to "prejudicial effect."

In fact the courts go in many directions, seldom with uniformity and often against criminal defendants as suggested by Footnote 56.[50]

---

[50]*See U.S. v. Brown*, 603 F.2d 1022 (1st Cir. 1979) (holding the district court did not abuse its discretion in allowing evidence of the defendant's outdated convictions under FRE 609(b) as the probative value of the evidence substantially outweighed its prejudicial effect where the government's witness' credibility was pitted against the defendant's credibility); *see also U.S. v. Gilbert*, 668 F. 2d 94 (2d Cir. 1981) (holding the trial judge did not abuse his discretion in ruling the defendant's mail fraud conviction that was over ten years old would have been admissible under FRE 609(b) had the defendant testified at his trial for violations of the federal securities laws because the prejudicial effect of the evidence did not outweigh the probative value); *U.S. v. Spero*, 625 F.2d 779 (8th Cir. 1980) (holding the trial court did not err under FRE 609(b) in allowing the government to cross-examine the defendant about his twenty-two-year-old grand theft conviction because the probative value of the conviction substantially outweighed its prejudicial effect and where credibility was an important question and defense counsel was allowed to cross-examine a government witness about the witness' outdated conviction); *United States v. Murray*, 751 F. 2d 1528 (9th Cir. 1985) (holding the trial court did not abuse its discretion under FRE 609(b) in admitting evidence of a bankruptcy fraud defendant's 1966 conviction for receiving stolen property as the probative value outweighed the possible prejudicial effect where the issue of credibility was important and the defense counsel was allowed considerable latitude in seeking to impeach the government witness); *United States v. Halbert*, 668 F.2d 489 (10th Cir. 1982) (holding the trial court could reasonably have determined under FRE 609(b) that the probative value of the defendant's prior bank robbery conviction outweighed its prejudicial effect where the defendant's credibility was issue); *United States v. Pritchard*, 973 F.2d 905 (11th Cir. 1992) (holding the trial court had not abused its discretion in admitting evidence of the defendant's remote burglary conviction after applying the balancing test mandated by FRE 609(b) where the defendant's credibility was a central issue at trial; *but cf. United States v. Beahm* 664 F.2d 414 (4th Cir. 1981) (holding

(continued)

Conversely, as suggested by Footnote 50, prosecution witnesses are, for the most part, favored by the courts. How, we might ask, are these witnesses prejudicially affected, save for some personal embarrassment that would not have a major impact on "... the interests of justice?"

Though seldom raised as an issue, it would appear the "remoteness" limitation applies to 609(a)(2) "dishonesty and false statement" crimes. *U.S. v. Cathey*, 591 F.2d 268 (5th Cir. 1979). Still we would imagine the nature of the crime, more specifically its relationship, if any, to credibility would be a factor determining "probative value."

Not Collateral

Rule 608, Truthfulness Impeachment, tells us it is always "collateral" impeachment and no extrinsic evidence may be used to prove the impeachment. There is no similar provision in Rule 609 which makes much sense.

Should a witness deny the existence of a conviction, you should be prepared to perfect your impeachment with a certified copy of the conviction. Obviously this would increase your impact score for now the convicted witness would add "liar" to his resume.

What If Your Opponent "Removes the Sting?"

As earlier mentioned, the proponent of a witness may impeach their own witness (FRE 607).

(footnote continued from previous page)
evidence of a defendant's eleven-year-old conviction for an offense similar to the one he was charged with should have been excluded under FRE 609(b) because the prejudicial effect of the evidence outweighed its probative value); *United States v. Cathey*, 591 F.2d 268 (5th Cir. 1979) (reversing the defendant's conviction for federal income tax evasion because the trial court abused its discretion under FRE 609(b) in finding the probative value of the defendant's outdated military conviction of larceny substantially outweighed its prejudicial effect and admitting evidence of the conviction); *United States v. Sims*, 588 F.2d 1145 (6th Cir. 1978) (reversing a defendant's conviction for being a felon in possession of a firearm because the trial court erred in determining, under FRE 609(b) that the probative value of the defendant's outdated convictions substantially outweighed its probative value, and in admitting evidence of the conviction); *United States v. Shapiro*, 565 F.2d 479 (7th Cir. 1977) (holding the trial court erred in admitting the defendant's over-twenty-year-old conviction into evidence under 609(b) because the probative value of the evidence clearly did not substantially outweigh its prejudicial effect); *United States v. Bensimon*, 172 F.3d 1121 (9th Cir. 1999) (holding the trial court abused its discretion where it admitted into evidence the defendant's seventeen-year-old conviction for mail fraud to impeach the defendant's testimony he was a good citizen and a religious family man).

An argument could be made that you will reduce the impact of 609 Conviction Impeachment (or, for that matter, other methods of impeachment) by fronting this information yourself. The phrase usually associated with this offensive action is you will "remove the sting."

Can your opponent "remove the sting?" By and large the answer is yes, though those judges who still consider "surprise" as a requirement to impeaching your own witness may not allow it.

In any event, should your opponent "remove the sting" you should nonetheless perfect your conviction impeachment your way, which as you will now see will differ greatly from how your opponent went about it.

How to Impeach With a Conviction

We start by telling you how not to impeach with a conviction:

Q: "Are you the same John Smith who was convicted of robbery in 2000 and received a sentence of five years?"

A: "Yes."

Unfortunately, this is the way many of us were taught to do it. Yet we know, if we put our minds to it, that it carries with it the excitement and impact of a-month-old newspaper.

Conviction impeachment is too powerful, too impactful, to waste it with "legal speak."

This would be a good time to recall that good trial lawyers "tell stories" and do not give "briefs" or use "legal speak."

It is also a good time to recall the importance of "primacy" in cross-examination. Usually, the *very best* primacy a trial lawyer could have would be conviction impeachment. Let us use it as such.

The witness has completed his direct examination. You start your cross-examination, obviously, with primacy.

Q: "It would be fair to say you are a convicted felon?"[51]

---

[51]Using somewhat different language, the prosecutor in the second trial of former Illinois Governor Blagojevich did just that. The papers and legal commentators considered it extremely effective. The statement made on cross examination was: "You are a convicted liar, correct?" Blagojevich answered: "Yes."

You may at this point, having accomplished your primacy, wish to go someplace else in your cross-examination and return to the guts of the conviction impeachment later in your cross-examination. Or, of course, you may wish to complete the conviction impeachment right from the "get-go."

Q: "As a matter of fact, you have been convicted of more than one felony?"
A: "Yes."
Q: "You have been convicted of two felonies?"
A: "Yes."
Q: "I want to ask you some questions about your first felony conviction, you understand?"
A: "Yes."

There are, understandably, some limitations on the scope of your conviction impeachment. Usually you are limited to eliciting the crime; most judges allow you to add a few details; the date of the crime and the date of the conviction; the place where the crime was committed; and the sentence. Obviously we will not exceed these limitations, but at the same time we will "milk" them and flower our "story" with other related facts and other methods of impeachment.

Q: "That was in 2004?"
A: "Yes."
Q: "February of 2004?"
A: "Yes."
Q: "February 5th?"
A: "Yes."
Q: "You robbed a 7-Eleven store?"
A: "Yes."
Q: "You were caught robbing the 7-Eleven store at 63rd Street and Western Avenue in Chicago?"
A: "Yes."
Q: "You were arrested?"
A: "Yes."

Q: "You were charged with armed robbery?"
A: "Yes."
Q: "You had a gun?"[52]
A: "Yes."
Q: "You pointed it at the store clerk?" (This may be objected to and the objection might be sustained.)
A: "Yes."
Q: "The police arrested you before you could escape?"
A: "Yes."
Q: "You were not happy you were caught?"
A: "Yes."

- Prosecutor: "OBJECTION, your Honor, this is not proper 609 impeachment.
- Defense: "Counsel is correct in suggesting this question would not be proper under 609 impeachment. It is not intended to be so. This is, however, proper motivation impeachment. I did start with 609 conviction impeachment and I will return to it shortly. In the meantime I will also use, as I should be allowed, motivation and also truthfulness impeachment.

Q: "You were not happy they caught you?"
A: "Yes."
Q: "You knew there was a good chance you would have to go to jail?"
A: "Yes."
Q: "You did not want to go to jail?"
A: "No."
Q: "You would do most anything to avoid going to jail?"
A: "Yes."
Q: "You ended up in a courtroom?"
A: "Yes."

---

[52]Picture trial advocacy. Make sure you hold up a gun, obviously your finger will do.

Q: "There was a judge there?"
A: "Yes."
Q: "You knew he would sentence you?"
A: "Yes."
Q: "As an armed robber?"
A: "Yes."
Q: "As a convicted felon?"
A: "Yes."
Q: "You did not want to go to jail?"
A: "No."
Q: "You wanted the shortest sentence possible?"
A: "Yes."
Q: "The judge told you that you could speak for yourself?"
A: "Yes."
Q: "You could give him reasons to either not put you in jail or to put you there for a shorter period of time?"
A: "Yes."
Q: "You were put under oath?"
A: "Yes."
Q: "Under oath, you promised the judge you would never commit another armed robbery?"
A: "Yes."
Q: "We now know you were not *truthful* with the judge?"
A: "Yes."
Q: "You lied to him?"
A: "Yes."
Q: "You lied to him for a reason?"
A: "Yes."
Q: "You lied to him to help yourself?"
A: "Yes."
Q: "The judge did sentence you as a *convicted felon*?"
A: "Yes."
Q: "You were sentenced as a *convicted felon* on September 6, 2004?"
A: "Yes."

Q: "On September 6, 2004, you were sentenced as a *convicted felon* to three years in prison?"[53]

A: "Yes."

Q: "On September 6, 2004, you went to prison?"

A: "Yes."

Q: "You did not enjoy the time you spent in prison?"

A: "No."

Q: "You would do most anything to avoid going back to prison?"

A: "Yes."

Q: "You did get out of prison on September 6 of 2006?"

A: "Yes."

Q: "You were still under a parole sentence?"

A: "Yes."

Q: "You were required to visit your parole officer?"

A: "Yes."

Q: "On the third Wednesday of each month?"

A: "Yes."

Q: "On those visits your parole officer always asked you if you had committed any crimes since he last saw you?"

A: "Yes."

Q: "You would always answer him?"

A: "Yes."

Q: "You always answered him 'no'?"

A: "Yes."

Q: "I want to ask you some questions about your visit with your parole officer on the third Wednesday in February 2008, you understand?"

A: "Yes."

Q: "Your parole officer asked you if you had committed any crimes since you last saw him?"

A: "Yes."

Q: "You told him you had not?"

A: "Yes."

---

[53]Note, "convicted felon" was "looped" three times.

Q: "But that answer was not accurate?" (The following would be truthfulness impeachment.)
A: "No."
Q: "It was not truthful?"
A: "No."
Q: "It was a lie?"
A: "Yes."
Q: "You lied for a reason?"
A: "Yes."
Q: "You lied to help yourself?"
A: "Yes."
Q: "You knew if you told the truth you could be put back in jail?"
A: "Yes."
Q: "You lied by not telling him about your having sold cocaine the first week of February?"
A: "Yes."
Q: "Now I want to ask you some questions about your second felony conviction, you understand?"
A: "Yes."

Now do the second felony conviction.

Applying What We Have Learned

A recent article in our local Chicago newspaper caught our attention. Under the heading "State DNA Analyst Admits Pay Theft," we are told a state criminal DNA analyst was caught having filed false overtime pay claims for $2,400.

Prosecutors had a problem. The analyst had done tests in hundreds of criminal cases, many of them still pending cases. In an all-too-obvious attempt to protect the analyst from impeachment in the pending cases (there may have been humanitarian reasons as well), the prosecutor, with unusual speed, allowed the analyst to plead guilty to misdemeanor theft of less than $300. She was sentenced to eighteen months of court supervision. The prosecutors suggested its action would allow the analyst to testify in the pending cases. Obviously, even if she had been convicted of the felony, she could still testify in the cases. Apparently the prosecutor was of the mind that their lenient treatment of the analyst would protect her from 609 impeachment.

Faulty, but apparently effective thinking.

The article concludes by noting local criminal defense attorneys were not pleased with how the case was handled. More specifically, they said that in the absence of a felony conviction they would be unable to impeach the analyst.

Had both the prosecutors and the criminal defense lawyers read this book the results might have been different. In the first instance the prosecutors, if they wanted, could charge the felony that was committed, knowing it would make no difference on the potential of trial impeachment.

More to the point, the criminal defense attorneys would know they were not precluded from impeaching the analyst – indeed, hopefully, some of them may have figured this out and impeached the analyst.

The facts suggest the availability of no less than three acceptable and proper methods of impeachment.

1. 609 – Conviction: Filing false overtime claims would apparently qualify as a misdemeanor involving "dishonesty and false statement."
2. 608 – Truthfulness: She obviously lied in filing her false claims. Any question about the applicability of 608 is quickly resolved in a reading of *U.S. v. Mansky*, 186 F.3d 770 (7th Cir. 1999).
3. Motivation: She was appearing as a prosecution witness. The prosecutor reduced a felony charge against her to a misdemeanor. Not only would this be proper motivation impeachment but were it denied to the defense you should have reversible error.

CHAPTER 6

What the Witness Could Have Done But Did Not Do

Obviously this method of impeachment is not supported by a specific rule of evidence. Rather it is, as are several other methods of impeachment, supported and justified by commonsense.

This method of impeachment is particularly effective when you cross-examine an expert witness.

Executing this method of impeachment requires some, but in truth little, care.

Again, as a trial lawyer you want to communicate your "story," your message, to the jury. You can best do this by "milking" this method of impeachment.

For example, you could simply impeach with

Q: "You did not tell Mr. Jones about the problem?"
A: "No."

Again we could and should push the envelope and milk this to better develop our story.

Q: "I want to ask you some questions about the problem you discovered on October 16th of last year, you understand?"
A: "Yes."
Q: "We can agree this was a major problem?"
A: "Yes."
Q: "This problem was of much concern to you?"
A: "Yes."
Q: "It was an important problem?"
A: "Yes."
Q: "It was a problem Mr. Jones would like to know about?"
A: "Yes."
Q: "This would have been of concern to him?"
A: "Yes."
Q: "This would have been of importance to him?"
A: "Yes."
Q: "But you did not tell him about the problem?"
A: "No."
Q: "You did not go see him to tell him about the problem?"
A: "No."
Q: "You did not call him on the telephone to tell him about this problem?"
A: "No."
Q: "You did not send him an e-mail to tell him about this important problem?"
A: "No."
Q: "You decided not to let him know about this important problem?"
A: "Yes."
Q: "Up until two months ago he did not know of this important problem?"
A: "Yes."
Q: "He did not know because you did not tell him?"
A: "Yes."

As mentioned, experts are susceptible to this method of impeachment.

Q: "I want to ask you some questions about what you did to prepare your report, you understand?"

A: "Yes."
Q: "You wanted to get all of the facts?"
A: "Yes."
Q: "You needed all of the facts?"
A: "Yes."
Q: "You certainly wanted to know all of the important facts?"
A: "Yes."
Q: "You wanted to know as much about Tim O'Brien as you could find out?"
A: "Yes."
Q: "This was important to you?"
A: "Yes."
Q: "You needed this important information to properly prepare your report?"
A: "Yes."
Q: "You wanted to know about his childhood?"
A: "Yes."
Q: "You wanted to know how he was raised?"
A: "Yes."
Q: "You wanted to know how he grew up?"
A: "Yes."
Q: "You knew he was raised by his mother and father?"
A: "Yes."
Q: "And you knew who they were?"
A: "Yes."
Q: "You knew he had a brother and sister?"
A: "Yes."
Q: "You knew who they were?"
A: "Yes."
Q: "You knew his parents would know more than anybody about how he grew up?"
A: "Yes."
Q: "You knew his brother and sister would know a great deal about how he grew up?"
A: "Yes."

Q: "Together, they would be the best source of information on how Tim O'Brien grew up?"
A: "Yes."
Q: "But you did not go see his mother?"
A: "No."
Q: "You did not call his mother on the phone?"
A: "No."
Q: "In no way did you tell his mother you wanted to talk to her?"
A: "No."
Q: "In fact you never talked to her?"
A: "No."
Q: "You did not go see his father?"
A: "No."
Q: "You did not call his father on the phone?"
A: "No."
Q: "In no way did you tell his father you wanted to talk to him?"
A: "No."
Q: "In fact you never talked to him?"
A: "No."
Q: "You did not go see his brother?"
A: "No."
Q: "You did not call his brother on the phone?"
A: "No."
Q: "In no way did you tell his brother you wanted to talk to him?"
A: "No."
Q: "In fact you never talked to him?"
A: "No."
Q: "You did not go see his sister?"
A: "No."
Q: "You did not call his sister on the phone?"
A: "No."
Q: "In no way did you tell his sister you wanted to talk to her?"
A: "No."
Q: "In fact you never talked to her?"
A: "No."

Q: "You never talked to any member of his family?"
A: "No."
Q: "You never talked to anybody with whom he grew up?"
A: "No."
Q: "You never talked to any of the people who would best know how Tim O'Brien grew up?"
A: "No."

Obviously there are many examples of "things not done." The witness did not call the police, did not go to a doctor, did not take pictures, did not take fingerprints or DNA examples.

To know the truth, what really happened, these things should have been done.

CHAPTER 7

Capacity

Were one to write a fiction novel involving a trial, usually a criminal trial, the method of impeachment most probably used would be capacity. This is so because capacity impeachment is most easily thought of and understood by nonlawyers or, as the case may be, non–trial lawyers. In truth and in fact, capacity impeachment is seldom available or used when compared to the methods of impeachment listed earlier.

Capacity impeachment is easy to define and explain and save, possibly, for one interesting evidence issue, is not difficult to understand. How to impeach with capacity is all too obvious and requires no explanation.

When using capacity impeachment you are challenging the witness's ability to perceive or recollect. You are challenging the witness's senses. In effect, you are suggesting the witness's ability to see, touch, taste, smell, or feel was defective.

As an aside, in the wonderful and entertaining movie *My Cousin Vinny* you will recall our criminal defense lawyer (the master of the opening statement!) Joe Pesci impeaching the witness with the "leaves." Because of the "leaves" the witness could not, suggests Pesci, have seen what he said he saw.

Again we have a method of impeachment not supported by its own rule of evidence. Capacity enjoys an all-too-obvious common law background and is based on common sense. *U.S. v. Cameron*, 814 F.2d 403 (7th Cir. 1987).

FRE Rule 701, which wisely expands the potential of lay witness opinion testimony, should likewise expand the potential of capacity impeachment. Recall, Rule 701(a) requires the nonexpert witness's opinion testimony be "rationally based on the witness's perception."

When the cross-examining attorney is establishing that it was "dark out" or that "the car was far away," or that the witness "did not have his glasses on," the cross-examining attorney is using capacity impeachment.

As suggested, capacity impeachment does, however, present an interesting and indeed important evidentiary issue.

As a cross-examiner, you would most welcome the opportunity to show the witness uses and abuses drugs (great bonus points), or (with fewer bonus points) that the witness is an alcoholic or has mental problems.

Can you use capacity impeachment to develop these points? It depends.

To use, as capacity impeachment, drug use, alcohol abuse, or mental problems, you must lay an understandable and obvious foundation. In a word, you must first show that the capacity problem either existed at the time of the event about which the witness testified, or exists now as the witness is on the stand.[54]

Absent one of these two required predicates, you will not be allowed to use this type of capacity impeachment.

Q: "I want to ask you some questions about what you were doing back in February of 2013, you understand?"
A: "Yes."
Q: "You were using drugs?"
A: "Yes."
Q: "You were drinking a lot?"
A: "Yes."
Q: "You were suffering from mental problems?"
A: "Yes."

---

[54]*See Smalley v. U.S.*, 798 F.2d 1182 (8th Cir. 1986); *U.S. v. Love*, 329 F. 3d 981 (8th Cir. 2003);

Q: "The drugs you were using were illegal drugs?" (Bonus points)
A: "Yes."
Q: "Occasionally they caused you to pass out?"
A: "Yes."
Q: "When you were stoned on drugs your ability to observe things was a problem?"
A: "Yes."
Q: "When you were stoned on drugs your ability to recall what had happened was a problem?"
A: "Yes."
Q: "When you were stoned on drugs your ability to relate to other people was a problem?"
A: "Yes."
Q: "During February 2013, there are things you don't remember?"
A: "Yes."
Q: "These problems were caused by your use of illegal drugs?"
A: "Yes."

Should the witness fight you on this line of questioning, the *collateral rule does not* apply. You may bring in witnesses (contradiction) to not only establish the capacity problem but also (bonus) show the witness to be a perjurer. (This assumes, of course, that the jury does not believe your witness is the one committing perjury!)

Refresher

Our obvious concern is to be able to show the jury the witness is a drug user. We see that this might be possible, assuming the proper foundation, as capacity impeachment.

Assume, however, we cannot establish the required foundation. What other methods of impeachment are possibly available to us?

- Rule 609 – Conviction as a Drug Crime
- Motivation – Probably your best bet in that this would probably be an uncharged crime.
- Rule 608 – Truthfulness: This might be a bit of a stretch unless, for instance, the witness was on parole and lied to his probation officer.

CHAPTER 8
FRE 404(b)

In truth, using 404(b) does not involve impeachment. It may, however, be used to attack and discredit a witness, and for that reason it is included with, albeit somewhat inaccurately, potential areas of impeachment.

Rule 404, more specifically Rule 404(a), deals with the use of character evidence. There is no reason for us to talk about how to use character evidence. Later we will cover the impeachment of a character witness.

Rule 404(b) starts, consistently with 404(a), with a disclaimer.

> **Prohibited Uses.** Evidence of a crime, wrong, or other act is not admissible to prove a person's character in order to show that on a particular occasion the person acted in accordance with the character.

This is understandable and makes much sense. We should convict a criminal defendant solely on the basis of the acts charged in the indictment, not on other bad acts they may have done.

As we continue to read 404(b) there is a major change in direction. We are introduced to a rule, not of exclusion, but of admission. To say the least it is a significant and potentially far-reaching rule of admission.

As the rule explains, crimes, wrongs, and acts (bad) may be admissible to prove motive, opportunity, intent, preparation, plan, knowledge, identity, or absence of mistake or accident, or, for that matter, whatever else one might think of. This list is not intended to be exclusive, and obviously the rule gives the trial judge discretion, which is seldom, if ever, exercised.

Rule 404(b) reads as follows:

> **(b) Crimes, wrongs or other acts.**
>
> **(1) Prohibited Uses.** Evidence of a crime, wrong, or other act is not admissible to prove a person's character in order to show that on a particular occasion the person acted in accordance with the character.
>
> **(2) Permitted Uses.** Notice in a Criminal Case. This evidence may be admissible for another purpose, such as proving motive, opportunity, intent, preparation, plan, knowledge, identity, absence of mistake, or lack of accident. On request by a defendant in a criminal case, the prosecutor must:
>
> **(A)** provide reasonable notice of the general nature of any such evidence that the prosecutor intends to offer at trial; and
>
> **(B)** do so before trial–or during trial if the court, for good cause, excuses lack of pretrial notice.

The "uncharged misconduct" admissible under Rule 404(b) need not, in and of itself, be a crime. Also, acts subsequent to those charged in the indictment may be included.

Rule 404(b) is subject to the balancing test of Rule 403, and may be excluded ". . . if it's probative value is substantially outweighed by the danger of unfair prejudice, confusion of the issues, or misleading the jury, or by considerations of undue delay, waste of time, or needless presentation of cumulative evidence."[55]

Rule 404(b) does require the prosecutor (recall this *notice requirement* does not apply to criminal defense lawyers or civil trial lawyers) give the defense "reasonable notice in advance of trial of the general nature of the evidence it intends to introduce," if "requested by the accused." Obviously the trial judge, "on good cause shown," may excuse the pretrial notice requirement.

Interestingly, before the rule was enacted prosecutors seldom, if ever, used this type of evidence. This was so notwithstanding the fact that the

---

[55]*Huddleston v. U.S.*, 485 U.S. 681 (1988).

rule did not create a new reason to admit evidence, it simply spelled out the common law.[56] What the rule did, however, was call this potential prosecution weapon to the attention of prosecutors, particularly federal prosecutors.

State prosecutors, on the other hand, could and did make use of rules particular to their state. For example, in New York, though obviously not in its federal courts, there was a broad right to impeach a witness on the basis of any "bad acts" they may have committed.[57] In Illinois, a witness may be impeached on the basis of an "unlawful and disreputable occupation."[58]

Back to Rule 404(b). The rule, albeit in a sophisticated way, seems to contradict itself. On the one hand, we are not allowed to introduce propensity evidence that would suggest a defendant (obviously it need not always be, but usually is, a criminal defendant) acted in conformity with the evidence. Then in the next breath we are told we may introduce Rule 404(b) evidence to show the defendant had, for instance, a motive, the opportunity, an intent, or plan related to the crime charged.[59]

Not surprisingly, Rule 404(b) is the most litigated of the Federal Rules of Evidence. As mentioned earlier, though not impeachment, prosecutors can, and do, successfully use Rule 404(b) to do damage to defendants. Criminal defendants[60] and civil trial lawyers[61] can also use the rule.

Criminal defense lawyers should read and know of *U.S. v. Montelongo*, 420 F.3d 1169 (10th Cir. 2005).

There can be little question, but that Rule 404(b) is the prosecutors' rule. The court in *Montelongo*, and indeed others, referred to "reverse 404(b) evidence" when a criminal defendant seek to use the rule. The trial court denied the defendants their attempt to cross-examine an important prosecution witness to suggest the witness, and not the defendants, had

---

[56] *People v. Molineux*, 168 N.Y. 264, 61 N.E. 286 1901; *Gianotos v. U.S.*, 104 F.2d 929 (9th Cir. 1939)

[57] *People v. Provenzano*, 435 N.Y.S. 2d. 369 (3rd Dep't 1980)

[58] *People v. Crump*, 5 Ill.2d 251 (1955); *People v. Garcia*, 90 Ill. App. 2d 396, 232 N.E.2d 810 (1967).

[59] See an excellent 404(b) opinion written by Judge Ann Williams of the Seventh Circuit reversing a conviction where Rule 404(b) evidence was improperly used. *U.S. v. Hicks*, 635 F.3d 1063 (7th Cir. 2011).

[60] *See U.S. v. James*, 169 F.3d 1210 (9th Cir. 1999)

[61] *Huddleston v. United States*, 485 U.S. 681, 685 (1988); *Barnes v. City of Cincinnati*, 401 F.3d 729 (7th Cir. 2005).

put the marijuana in the cab of the truck the defendants were driving. The cross-examination would have been predicated on Rule 404(b).

Having denied the cross-examination, the two defendants were convicted. The Tenth Circuit reversed the convictions. The opinion is well done and well worth reading. The opinion was predicated not only upon the denial of the defendants' right to cross-examine using Rule 404(b), but also on a Sixth Amendment Confrontation Clause violation.

Though this is not an evidence book, indeed there are many such excellent books available that cover this issue, we make brief mention of a "kissing cousin" to Rule 404(b), the "inextricably intertwined" doctrine. On occasion, albeit rare, courts have allowed "bad act" evidence where the evidence is "inextricably intertwined" with the elements of the crime charged. In a word, Rule 404(b) need not be used, nor would its notice requirement apply. The good news is this common law rule of evidence is being questioned and is out of favor. *United States v. Gorman*, 613 F.3d 711 (7th Cir. 2010).[62]

A fairly recent decision by the Iowa Supreme Court limits the "inextricably intertwined" doctrine to circumstances where "the charged and uncharged crimes wrongs or acts. . . form a continuous transaction." *State v. Nelson*, 791 N.W. 2d 414 (Iowa Dec. 10, 2010).[63]

In sum, though not true impeachment, the opportunities made available through Rule 404(b) present trial lawyers, in particular prosecutors, effective ways to attack a witness.[64]

---

[62]BNA Insights on Evidence (*Criminal Law Reporter* 4/20/11, Vol 89, No. 3 p. 99) contains an excellent article by Alain Leibman.

[63]See a thorough and well-written opinion on both Rule 404(b) and the "inextricably intertwined" doctrine by the Third Circuit in *U.S. v. Green*, 617 F.3d 233 (3d Cir. 2010). The court, in affirming a conviction, held that, as urged by the prosecutor, the "inextricably intertwined doctrine did not apply, but that Rule 404(b) did apply."

[64]Though seldom used by criminal defense lawyers, Rule 404(b), or a version of it, is available to them.

The Arizona Supreme Court presents us with an interesting opinion in *State v. Machado*, 246 P.3d 632 (2011). Defendant was on trial for the murder of a young female friend. The defense was that another friend of the young lady was the killer. To that end, the defense sought to introduce evidence the other fellow had threatened the woman. This was allowed. Also, evidence that the other fellow had kidnapped two other girls at gunpoint, and

(continued)

The Seventh Circuit, in an opinion written by Judge Evans, spells out its test as to the admissibility of Rule 404(b) evidence:

> We apply a four-part test to decide whether Rule 404(b) evidence was properly admitted and will find no error if: (1) the evidence is directed toward establishing a matter in issue other than the Defendant's propensity to commit the crime charged; (2) the evidence shows that the other act is similar enough and close enough in time to be relevant to the matter in issue; (3) the evidence is sufficient to support a jury finding that the Defendant committed the similar act; and (4) the evidence has probative value that is not substantially outweighed by the danger of unfair prejudice. *U.S. v. Vargas*, 552 F.3d 550, 554 (7th Cir. 2008).

(footnote continued from previous page)
had been convicted of pointing a fake gun at and telling a former girlfriend that he had killed before, was not allowed.

The Arizona Supreme Court, in reversing the conviction, held that "the admission of third-party culpability evidence is governed by the standards of Rules 401 through 403 of the Arizona Rules of Evidence, not by Rule 404(b)." *State v. Machado*, 226 Ariz. 281, 284 (2011).

This was not a 404(b) case, nor did it involve impeachment. Still it deserves mention.

CHAPTER 9

Habit

Evidence of a routine practice or as it is called a "habit" may be admissible on direct examination or on cross-examination to impeach the witness.

Rule 406 of the Federal Rules states as follows:

> Evidence of a person's habit or an organization's routine practice may be admitted to prove that on a particular occasion the person or organization acted in accordance with the habit or routine practice. The court may admit this evidence regardless of whether it is corroborated or whether there was an eyewitness.

Note the rule applies not only to individuals but to organizations as well: ". . . or an organization's routine practice . . ." For this reason, among others, the rule is used more in civil than in criminal cases.

Once again, we have a rule creating an exception similar to Rule 404(b), an exception to Rule 404's exclusion of character evidence.

Again we must distinguish "habits" from general character. This is a difficult distinction to make.

The rule does not make our task any easier in that the rule does not define "habit."

It is generally accepted that there are two, somewhat conflicting, theories governing the admissibility of "habit" evidence. The psychological theory is the more conservative of the theories.

To qualify the conduct must be nonvolitional, semi-automatic, and unconsciously mechanical. Basically, it must be an instinctual Pavlovian response.[65]

The more liberal probability theory simply requires a regular reflexive response to a (repeated) specific situation. Again, this would be a very subjective determination, one that moves us close to "character."

Neither the rule nor the congressional comments give much guidance to the courts. Then again this appears to be purposely so.

The Federal Rules of Evidence in general, even more specifically the "habit" Rule 406, purposely leave flexibility and much discretion to trial judges. Seldom, if ever, will a trial court ruling on "habit" be reversed.

The admissibility of "habit" evidence is subject to the "prejudice, confusion and waste of time" objection found in Rule 403. The Rule 403 limitation would suggest more reasons for a reversal than the basic Rule 406 ruling. See an excellent and thorough history of the Federal Rules of Evidence with emphasis on the philosophy and purpose of the Rules. "The Theory of Discretion with the Federal Rules of Evidence." 74 Iowa L.R. by Professor Thomas M. Mengler.

The Drafting Committee would have allowed "habit" to be proved by "opinion or specific instances." Congress eliminated this language and opted to leave discretion to this trial judge.

Not surprisingly the court opinions, actually there are few, are not necessarily uniform.

As mentioned earlier "habit" evidence is more probably used in civil trials. For example, a plaintiff's use or for that matter nonuse, of a seatbelt might well be the subject of habit evidence.

Habit evidence also finds its way into medical malpractice cases. See 87 *Marq. L. Rev.* 981 (Summer 2004).

---

[65]Pavlov rang a bell to alert dogs that he was bringing their food. The bell served as a stimulus which had the capacity to provoke a reflexive response.

Finally, legal scholars are of the opinion that "habit" evidence is highly probative and accordingly superior to character evidence (Rule 404). This may well be so in civil trials; however, our experience with "habit" and character evidence in a criminal trial would favor the impact of character over "habit" evidence.

In any event, though its infrequence of use and availability would have it low on our list of ways to impeach, one should be aware of its existence, particularly in civil cases.

The senior MacCarthy has vague recollection of using "habit" impeachment once many years ago. Actually the specific facts are, as they should be, lost.

The wording and letter of the rule were followed. Interestingly there was no objection by the prosecutor, nor did the trial judge express concern with the "habit" impeachment. These omissions should have been considered.

Upon the completion of the "habit" impeachment it was all too obvious it had little or no impact. For that matter the point made, whatever it was, was not even mentioned in the closing argument.

That said the situation might arise where "habit" impeachment might be helpful – particularly in civil cases.

CHAPTER 10

Writing Used to Refresh Memory

We have earlier, when talking of the law related to impeaching a witness with an inconsistent statement, made mention of a cross-examiner's right to refresh the memory of a witness who tells us they do not remember or recall something. We briefly explained when and how this could and should be done.

Now we learn that a witness whose memory has been refreshed creates a separate impeachment opportunity. Back in law school when taking our basic course in evidence, we were introduced to the two ugly sisters, "refreshing recollection" (as it was then called) and "past recollection recorded."[66]

Candor requires we admit that we never fully understood the two ugly sister rules. We tried, though they made little sense, to learn enough about them to make off we knew what we were talking about on the final exam

[66]Fed. R. Evid. 803(5): Recorded Recollection. A record that (a) is on a matter the witness once knew about but now cannot recall well enough to testify fully and accurately, (b) was made or adopted by the witness when the matter was fresh in the witness's memory, and (c) accurately reflects the witness's knowledge. If admitted, the record may be read into evidence but may be received as an exhibit only if offered by an adverse party.

and later when taking the bar examination. After the bar examination we washed them out of our mind, along with the Rule in Shelley's case.

Sounds about right, but now when we are or aspire to be trial lawyers we realize we must know and learn about these confusing ugly sisters. As bad as they appear, they may well be useful to us.

In truth, our evidence professors often added to our confusion. We suggest an interesting experiment. Ask a lawyer what they best remember about "refreshing recollection." (If you call it refreshing memory, you may confuse them big time.) Having done this, we have found the usual answer is "you can use anything to refresh recollection, it can be a rock or a building." (Sure, try and get the building, no less the rock if it is a large one, into the courtroom!)

Collectively we have lectured to thousands of trial lawyers on impeachment, and more specifically refreshing recollection or, if you wish, memory. We have made it a point to ask if any of them ever used anything other than a writing to refresh the recollection or memory. No one has responded affirmatively.

Little wonder we are confused.

Rule 612 of Federal Rules of Evidence tells us much, indeed most, of what we must know. Parenthetically the rule wisely reads, "Writing (no mention of a rock or whatever) Used to Refresh a Witness's Memory." The rule reads as follows:

> **Writing Used to Refresh a Witness's Memory.**
>
> (a) **Scope.** This rule gives an adverse party certain options when a witness uses a writing to refresh memory: (1) while testifying; or (2) before testifying, if the court decides that justice requires the party to have those options.
>
> (b) **Adverse Party's Options; Deleting Unrelated Matter.** Unless 18 U.S.C. § 3500 provides otherwise in a criminal case, an adverse party is entitled to have the writing produced at the hearing, to inspect it, to cross-examine the witness about it, and to introduce in evidence any portion that relates to the witness's testimony. If the producing party claims that the writing includes unrelated matter, the court must examine the writing in camera, delete any unrelated

portion, and order that the rest be delivered to the adverse party. Any portion deleted over objection must be preserved for the record.

(c) **Failure to Produce or Deliver the Writing.** If a writing is not produced or is not delivered as ordered, the court may issue any appropriate order. But if the prosecution does not comply in criminal case, the court must strike the witness's testimony or – if justice so requires – declare a mistrial.

From a reading of the rule we learn that there are two ways a witness might refresh their memory. As trial lawyers we should, in particular, be familiar with the far more common of the two ways, the witness having their memory refreshed while they are on the stand testifying. This can occur on either direct or cross-examination. To allow refreshing memory the witness must show that she does not recall or remember something she once knew, and that something (the rock!) would help remind her what it was.

As spelled out in Rule 612, we learn that a witness may also refresh their memory before testifying.

Obviously, before testifying most witnesses are prepared or, as often called, "woodshedded," before they appear on the stand. Understandably they often read reports and most often read earlier statements they have made.

Before the Federal Rules of Evidence there was little concern or authority to allow an opposing attorney to see or use what the witness read and reviewed before taking the stand.

The drafters of the Federal Rules of Evidence, we believe correctly, were of the view that the need to allow an opponent to see and use what was used to refresh recollection before the witness takes the stand, was as important and necessary as when the refreshing is done when the witness is actually on the stand.

The Congress, concerned about "fishing expeditions" among documents the witness may have read in preparing to testify, disagreed with the recommendation of the Advisory Committee.

A bit of a compromise was reached. Rule 612 does authorize the opposing attorney to see and introduce into evidence those documents used by the witness to refresh before taking the stand, but only where and if the trial judge finds that seeing and introducing the documents are "*. . . necessary in the interest of justice . . .*"

Obviously what is or what is not ". . . necessary in the interest of justice . . ." is a difficult standard to define or explain. That said, it would probably be fair to say that most judges presented with this issue, and in truth little guidance, err on the side of the pre-Federal Rules of Evidence and Congressional thinking.[67]

Occasionally a court will find the ". . . necessary in the interest of justice . . ." requirement. *United States v. Smith*, 521 F.2d 957 (D.C. Cir. 1975).

The fact that the document used to refresh is itself inadmissible does not affect its being used to refresh or your right to see and use it, though it will preclude it being admitted into evidence.[68]

If a document is used to refresh and it must be turned over, the claim that the document is protected by the attorney–client or, for that matter, any other privilege, will not protect it.[69]

In sum, where a witness has their memory refreshed while testifying, you are allowed to see the refreshing document, to cross-examine and, obviously, to impeach with the document. If the refreshing was done before the witness takes the stand, you would have to satisfy the trial judge that "it is necessary in the interest of justice" that you get to see and use the refreshing document.

There is still another "speed bump" in producing refreshing documents in federal criminal cases. Though, for common sense reasons, this "speed bump" is seldom followed to the letter.

The "speed bump" is the so-called Jencks Act (18 U.S.C. § 3500). It provides that in criminal cases pretrial statements of prosecution witnesses need not be disclosed until after the direct examination of that witness. Thus, the trial judge's right to require production under Rule 612 may be delayed until after the witness completes their direct examination.

---

[67]*See United States v. Sai Keung Wong*, 886 F.2d 252 (9th Cir. 1989); *Leucadia, Inc. v. Reliance Ins. Co.*, 101 F.R.D. 674 (S.D. N.Y. 1983); *United States v. Williams*, 875 F.2d 846 (11th Cir. 1989); *Cosden Oil & Chem. Co. v. Karl O. Helm A.G.*, 736 F.2d 1064 (5th Cir. 1984).

[68]*United States v. Scott*, 701 F.2d 1340 (11th Cir. 1983).

[69]*Marshall v. Postal Service*, 88 F.R.D. 348 (D.C.C. 1980); *Leybold-Heraeus Tech. Inc. v. Midwest Instrument Co.*, 118 F.R.D. 609 (E.D. Wisc. 1987).

The Jencks Act is limited to statements of the witness. If the refreshing document is not a statement of the witness it is not protected by the Jencks Act.

Civil trial lawyers and those few criminal defense lawyers who practice in jurisdictions that allow depositions should be aware that Rule 612 applies to depositions.[70]

One final, albeit important, suggestion. Before a trial lawyer is allowed to refresh recollection or memory during trial, the lawyer must, according to some trial judges, have the witness allow that she does not recall or remember. The witness must further allow that the document would refresh her recollection or memory.

This chapter involves much evidence law and little trial advocacy. Still the point is made that Rule 612 creates the potential for impeachment.

One of us had the issue come up. The circumstance and indeed the impact were unusual. During lunch we ran into the prosecutor's expert witness. Knowing him and having cross-examined him before, we struck up a brief conversation. To clarify a minor point we asked him a question about his expected testimony. He responded in a polite and professional way by explaining that the prosecutor did not want him to talk to us. This, in and of itself, would be a "no-no" and would probably constitute reversible error.[71] We asked him when the prosecutor told him this. His answer was, to say the least, most interesting. He said he was so instructed in a detailed letter the prosecutor had written him where the prosecutor told him what he wanted him to testify to.

One final statement. You read this letter to prepare for your testimony today. He answered he had.

---

[70] *James Julian Inc. v. Raytheon Co.*, 93 F.R.D. 138 (D. Del. 1982).

[71] The defense does not have the right to interview the prosecution witnesses, an accurate but questionable conclusion. The witness has the right not to be interviewed by the defense.

On the other hand, the defense does have the right to be free from interference by the prosecutor in the witnesses' right or choice. Simply stated a prosecutor may explain to a witness that they have the right to talk to or not talk to the defense. The prosecutor may not, however, recommend, advise, or suggest the witness they not talk to the defense. *U.S. v. Troutman*, 814 F.2d 1428, 1453-54, *U.S. v. Pinto*, 755 F.2d 150, 152 (10th Cir. 1985); (10th Cir. 1987); *Gregory v. U.S.*, 369 F.2d 185 (D.C. Cir. 1966).

Q: "I want to ask you some questions about a letter the prosecutor sent you, you understand?"
(Obviously the prosecutor objected to this question. And obviously the trial judge overruled the objection.)
A: "Yes."
Q: "First off, the prosecutor told you not to talk to us?"
A: "Yes."
Q: "And for that reason you would not talk with us about your testimony?"
A: "Yes."
Q: "If the prosecutor had not told you not to talk to us, you would have?"
A: "Yes."
Q: "The prosecutor's letter not only told you what not to do, but also told you what to do?"
A: "Yes."
Q: "More specifically, he told you what he wanted you to say?"
A: "Yes."

The exceptionally able trial judge had no problem finding the letter should be produced as being "necessary in the interest of justice."

In truth and in fact, the impact of the impeachment was directed more to the prosecutor than the witness. To say the least it was effective.

CHAPTER 11
An Opposing Party's Statement

(or What Some Still Refers to as an Admission)

This method of impeachment is spelled out in the Federal Rules of Evidence.

The point could be made that what we called admissions are the same as inconsistent statements. There is much similarity, but there are also a few distinguishing differences.

The Federal Rules of Evidence spell out opposing party statements impeachment in the hearsay definition Rule FRE 801. Subsection (d) of the rule tells us what statements are not hearsay. An opposing party's statement is *not* hearsay; Rule 801(d) tells us

> A statement that meets the following conditions is not hearsay:
>
> (1) **A Declarant-Witness's Prior Statement.** The declarant testifies and is subject to cross-examination about a prior statement, and the statement: (A) is consistent with the declarant's testimony and was given under penalty of perjury at a trial, hearing, or other proceeding or in a deposition; (B) is consistent with the declarant's

> testimony and is offered to rebut an express or implied charge that the declarant recently fabricated it or acted from a recent improper influence or motive in so testifying or (C) identifies a person as someone the declarant perceived earlier.
>
> (2) **An Opposing Party's Statement.** The statement is offered against an opposing party and: (A) was made by the party in an individual or representative capacity; (B) is one the party manifested that it adopted or believed to be true; (C) was made by a person whom the party authorized to make a statement on the subject; (D) was made by the party's agent or employee on a matter within the scope of that relationship and while it existed; or (E) was made by the party's coconspirator during and in furtherance of the conspiracy.
>
> The statement must be considered but does not by itself establish the declarant's authority under (C); the existence or scope of the relationship under (D); or the existence of the conspiracy or participation in it under (E).

Recall again the relatively broad definition of the term "statement." A statement is ". . . a person's oral assertion, written assertion, or nonverbal conduct, if the person intended it as an assertion." (FRE 801(a)).

In civil cases they can be and are used to hold an employer liable for the actions of an employee. The obvious example would be the use of the employee driver's statement made after the collision: "I am sorry I ran the light." A far more potential source of opposing party statements would be the complaint, the answer; in a word, the pleadings.

In criminal trials, these statements are occasionally used against criminal defendants[72] but are seldom, for questionable reasons, used against the prosecution.

United States v. McKeon, 738 F.2d 26, 31 (2d Cir. 1984) is an interesting, albeit possibly far-reaching, case involving such statements. During the opening statement in a criminal case in the Federal District Court, the criminal defense attorney told the jury he would prove that important photocopies the prosecutor would introduce into evidence were not, as the prosecutor had said in his opening statement, reproduced on the photocopy machine where the defendant's wife worked.

---

[72]*United States v. Carrasco*, 540 F. 3d 43 (9th Cir. 2008).

The defense delivered on this promise by calling an expert on photocopies (yes, apparently there are such people) who opined that the photocopies were not made on the photocopier where the defendant's wife worked.

Apparently this helped the defense. The jury hung.

Before the second trial the defense expert ran into his professor, the one who had taught him and in effect made him an expert. In pleasantly catching up with each other the professor mentioned that he was going to testify in a criminal trial in the federal court. He was going to be a prosecution witness and testify that photocopies *were* made on the photocopy machine in the office where the defendant's wife worked.

Thought the young expert made no mention to his professor of his involvement in the same case, he immediately told the criminal defense lawyer of his meeting and conversation. They both agreed that the professor would be the more experienced, knowledgeable, and accepted expert. The young expert would not be a witness in the second trial.

Obviously the criminal defense lawyer, experienced and deservedly well regarded, changed his opening statement. With commendable, as well as necessary, candor he admitted the photocopies were made on the photocopy machine in the office where the defendant's wife worked.

The prosecution, using much imagination and "pushing the envelope," argued to the jury in closing that the defense was guilty of speaking out of both sides of its mouth. More specifically, they told the jury that the defendant's attorney had told the jury in the *first trial* that they would prove the photocopies were not made in the defendant's wife's office. The prosecutors argued, successfully, that counsel's opening statement in the first trial was, as it was then called, an admission.

The defendant, not surprisingly, was convicted and the Second Circuit affirmed the conviction. *U.S. v. McKeon*, 738 F.2d 26, 31 (2d Cir. 1984).

There is, however, one major limitation on the use of such statements. The limitation applies to criminal defendants. Using somewhat archaic and faulty reasoning, some courts severely limit the use by criminal defendants of such statements against the prosecutors.

Apparently relying on, if not actually mentioning, the "divine right of Kings" (which we understood was put to rest by the Magna Carta), courts have held that "no individual can bind the sovereign." *U.S. v. Pervatta*,

16 F.3d 763 (7th Cir. 1994). This reasoning continues with the questionable suggestion that government people are "disinterested in the outcome" of cases.

For the most part then, when this philosophy prevails, criminal defendants are precluded from using such statements against government employees such as FBI agents, informers, as well as matters contained in government publications.[73]

Interestingly, *U.S. v. Dehoach*, 34 F.3d 1001, 1005 (11th Cir. 1994) stands in stark contrast to the opinion of the Second Circuit in *McKeon*. The Eleventh Circuit concluded the prosecutor's closing argument was not admissible as an admission.

On a positive note, the limitation on the use of admissions by criminal defendants is being questioned, challenged, and corrected.[74]

Under certain circumstances, where there may not be an "admission" but rather plea negotiations, the prosecutor understandably remains protected. More specifically, in *U.S. v. Delgado*, 903 F.2d 1495, 1499 (11th Cir. 1990) the court held a prosecutor's statements in plea agreements are not admissions. The prosecutor did not necessarily believe the defendant was innocent of the dropped charges.

From the case law we distill the following:

1. The opposing party's statement can be of fact, opinion, or conclusions of law or fact, and need not be based on personal knowledge.
2. The declarant of the statement need not testify at trial.
3. There is no guarantee of trustworthiness required.
4. Obviously, these statements are subject to relevancy requirements.

Importantly admissions, unlike inconsistent statements, always come in as substantive evidence.[75]

---

[73]*See U.S. v. Finley*, 705 F. Supp. 1297 (N.D. Ill. 1988); *U.S. v. McKeon*, 738 F.2d 26, 31 (2d Cir. 1984).

[74]In *U.S. v. Morgan*, 581 F.2d 933, 937, 938 (D.C. Cir. 1978) the prosecutor's sworn affidavit for a search warrant was an indication the prosecutor believed the statement trustworthy; this qualifying it as an admission. In *U.S. v. Branham*, 97 F.3d 835, 851 (6th Cir. 1996) the court held that an informant's conversations with the defendant were admissions. Also, the Ninth Circuit held that a government manual was admissible as an admission. *U.S. v. VanGriffin*, 874 F. 2d 634 (9th Cir. 1989).

[75]*Vogel v. Percy*, 691 F. 2d 843 (7th Cir. 1982); *U.S. v. Cisneros-Gutierrez*, 517 F.3d 751 (5th Cir. 2008).

CHAPTER 12

Hearsay Declarant

Yes, you can actually impeach someone who may never testify as a witness. Rule 806 of the Federal Rules of Evidence reads as follows:

> **Attacking and supporting the declarant credibility.** When a hearsay statement – or a statement described in Rule 801(d)(2) (C), (D), or (E) – has been admitted in evidence, the declarant's credibility may be attacked, and then supported, by any evidence that would be admissible for those purposes if the declarant had testified as a witness. The court may admit evidence of the declarant's inconsistent statement or conduct, regardless of when it occurred or whether the declarant had an opportunity to explain or deny it. If the party against whom the statement was admitted calls the declarant as a witness, the party may examine the declarant on the statement as if on cross-examination.

In truth, the rule is little known and seldom used. Unfortunately, when used, it is often misunderstood and misinterpreted.[76] Some of the

[76]An all-too-obvious example of not knowing Rule 806 is spelled out in the Fifth Circuit opinion in *U.S. v. Moody*, 903 F.2d 321 (5th Cir. 1990). Two codefendants decided not to stay around to be tried. The prosecutor properly used their inculpatory hearsay statements *(continued)*

problems with the rule are caused by the failure of the drafters to better spell out what they intended and how it should work. Most of the confusion is caused by a failure to understand the rule. Trial lawyers and judges could use additional clarification and guidance, and they could and should learn more about the rule.

Simply stated, Rule 806 tells us we can impeach the declarant of a hearsay statement or hearsay conduct, and even some things that are nonhearsay. We can impeach them as we would if we were cross-examining the declarant.

The rule is necessary and well intended. The hearsay declarant[77] has said or written something that hurts your case. It is only fair that you should have this right to impeach the source of the hurt, the declarant.[78]

The rule applies to both criminal and civil cases, though in truth most of the issues and case law concerns criminal cases. Again, the rule is not well-known nor its potential appreciated.

As mentioned, the rule is, for the most part, directed at hearsay statements. It follows that these hearsay statements come into evidence as one of the exceptions to the hearsay rule. The statement or evidence comes in to prove its truth. Obviously then the credibility of the declarant may be an issue and should be and is subject to impeachment as if the declarant had testified.[79]

The problem, of course, is the declarant may not, indeed usually does not, testify as a witness.

This can and does create problems.

(footnote continued from previous page)
to incriminate the defendant Moody. Commendably, Moody's lawyer knew of and sought to use Rule 806 to impeach the absent codefendant's reputation for truthfulness (Rule 608). The prosecutor objected with arguments that demonstrated that he was obviously unfamiliar with Rule 806. The trial court summarily sustained the objection. The Court of Appeals properly reversed.

[77]The rule, for the most part, applies to admissible hearsay. But as earlier mentioned, it can also apply to nonhearsay.

[78]In a sound and helpful opinion, the Fifth Circuit held that a denial of the Rule 806 right to impeach violated the defendant's Sixth Amendment Confrontational Clause right. *United States v. Moody*, 903 F.2d 321 (5th Cir. 1990) (holding the denial of FRE 806 right to impeach violated the defendant's Sixth Amendment Confrontational Clause right); *see also Delaware v. Van Arsdall*, 475 U.S. 673, 678-79 (1986) (announcing Sixth Amendment confrontational guarantee to cross and impeach motivations of adversarial witnesses).

[79]*See* specifically FRE 803, 804, 805, and 807.

Obviously in criminal cases who introduces the Rule 806 statement becomes important. In that the case law, for the most part, concerns itself with criminal cases we will do likewise.

The defendant may introduce the Rule 806 statement, clearly an exculpatory statement favorable to the defendant. Most likely this strategy might be used where the defendant, were he to testify, would be subject to impeachment, most likely impeachment with a crime under Rule 609. The defendant, it would appear, need not testify but could still get in the favorable evidence. Defendants beware!

Still another possibility might arise where the defense is insanity and the defendant's statements to his psychiatrist might be helpful. FRE 803(4) specifically created a hearsay exception for statements made for the purposes of medical diagnosis or treatment. This is a frequent practice in defending insanity cases. There is a potential problem however where the defendant would be subject to impeachment, particularly with a Rule 609 conviction. Obviously the prosecutor could use Rule 806 to impeach.[80]

At first blush this seems to make sense, and would if it were not for Rule 806.

The case law is both clear and understandable. The nontestifying defendant who introduces his own hearsay statement subjects himself to Rule 806 impeachment.[81]

Is there a way for the nontestifying defendant to get the helpful statement (usually a denial of knowing anything about the crime) into evidence without subjecting himself to impeachment?

Yes, but again there are serious risks. The defense, if at all possible, may request the statement be admitted not as admissible hearsay for the truth of what is said but merely as a "verbal act." If it comes into evidence not as admissible hearsay, but as a "verbal act," Rule 806 may not apply. Support for this distinction can be found in cases where the prosecutor introduced the statement and the trial court did not allow Rule 608

[80] *See U.S. v. Lechoco*, 542 F.2d 84 (D.C. Cir. 1976).

[81] *See U.S. v. Newman*, 849 F.2d 156 (5th Cir. 1988), *U.S. v. Noble*, 754 F.2d 1324 (7th Cir. 1985) – unrelated to this issue, Senior MacCarthy is mentioned (p. 1333) in the opinion; *U.S. v. Lawson*, 608 F. 2d 1129 (6th Cir. 1979).

impeachment, finding that the statement was not hearsay, but merely a "verbal act."[82]

There remains a potential problem if the statement is introduced not by the defendant, but rather by the prosecutor or a codefendant. This would take us into murky waters.

Obviously a prosecutor would welcome introducing a defendant's statement, particularly one that is not particularly damaging, where the nontestifying defendant is impeachable, most obviously and preferably, by a Rule 609 conviction.

The temptation to do this can cause problems, but may not be as bad as this may seem. There is a basic agreement that a prosecutor may not call a witness for the sole purpose of impeaching the defendant through the use of Rule 806.[83]

That said, we can and should expect courts to look for valid reasons, apart from the opportunity to impeach the defendant, for calling the witness. *U.S. v. Peterman*, 841 F.2d 1474 (10th Cir. 1988) is such a case. The witness was convicted in an earlier trial. In a second trial the prosecutor called him as a witness. When he testified favorably to the defendant, the prosecutor impeached him with his earlier conviction. Importantly, this was not a Rule 806 impeachment. Defendant objected in that the conviction was basically the case against defendant.

The issue presented to the court was what exactly did the prosecutor expect the witness to say? The witness said he had told the prosecutor what his testimony would be. The prosecutor said he believed the witness would now change his earlier trial testimony and now admit to committing the crime. (So much for "woodshedding the witness" and knowing what his testimony would be!)

Understandably, the court of appeals was not impressed with the defendant's argument.

---

[82]*See U.S. v. Zagari et. al.*, 111 F.3d 307 (2d Cir. 1997); *U.S. v. Davis*, 890 F.2d 1373 (7th Cir. 1989); *U.S. v. Becerra*, 992 F.2d 960 (9th Cir. 1993); *U.S. v. McClain*, 943 F.2d 822 (7th Cir. 1991)

[83]*See U.S. v. Silverstein*, 737 F. 2d 864 (10th Cir. 1984); *U.S. v. Webster*, 734 F. 2d 1191 (1984).

The prosecutor additionally represented that he and the DEA special agent had met with the witness before he testified and, based on that meeting (the "woodshedding"), they expected him to admit his involvement in the crime. Obviously, the witness and the prosecutor could not both be telling the truth. The court gave the nod to the prosecutor and the special agent rather than to the convicted felon. The court believed the prosecutor was surprised by the testimony and thus the impeachment was proper.

In *U.S. v. Bovain*, 708 F.2d 606 (11th Cir. 1983) the Eleventh Circuit wrote an interesting, if not fully understandable, opinion. Again, the prosecutor in a multidefendant conspiracy trial introduced Rule 806 material through the testimony of a cooperating coconspirator. Hearsay statements of nontestifying defendant, Finch, were mentioned. The statements implicated still another codefendant, Rickett, who availed himself of Rule 806 to impeach Finch with 609 convictions involving stolen money orders and narcotics.[84]

Viewed by the language of Rule 806, this impeachment (at least the stolen money order conviction) should have been allowed.

The problem, however, is the potential, though it is not clearly spelled out, of a conflict with Rule 609. Rule 609 was intended to protect defendants who do not testify from being impeached with criminal convictions.[85]

Regardless of who introduces the Rule 806 hearsay, impeachment might also be sought, as was the circumstance in *Bovain*, by a codefendant. Particularly where the impeachment takes the form of a Rule 609 criminal conviction, we have, as mentioned, the problem of a possible conflict with Rule 609.

The trial court was obviously aware of and concerned with this problem in *U.S. v. Robinson*, 783 F.2d 64 (7th Cir. 1986).

---

[84]This was a narcotics trial. The extreme prejudice of the narcotic conviction strongly suggests it should not have been allowed. This issue is not mentioned. To further confuse matters, the trial court denied Rickett the right to impeach Finch's convictions for forgery and escape.

[85]See "Evidence Rule 806 and the Problem of Impeaching the Non-Testifying Declarant," 56 *Ohio St. L.J.* 496, an excellent article by Professor Margaret Meriwether Cordray.

Anticipating the problem, the defendants sought severance. This was denied, and the Seventh Circuit agreed with this ruling. The trial judge, rather interestingly, would not allow Rule 806 impeachment of any of the defendants. Again the Seventh Circuit agreed.

In *U.S. v. Lebnfesty*, 923 F.2d 1293 (8th Cir. 1989) the trial judge in effect "cut the baby in half." Rule 608 Truthfulness Impeachment was allowed, but the judge denied Rule 609 impeachment with felony convictions. The conviction was affirmed.

Two final legal issues. When Rule 806 evidence has been used against you, you have the right to call the declarant and cross-examine.[86] Where possible, this is something that should be considered for the reasons to be discussed involving the limitations on Rule 806 impeachment where the declarant is not on the stand.

Finally, the party offering the Rule 806 testimony may rehabilitate the declarant.[87]

How to Impeach Using Rule 806

We have struggled through much confusing and contradictory case law. Accepting, as we can best understand it, Rule 806, the question now becomes how do we, as trial lawyers, use it.

Let us start with the suggestion that impeachment using Rule 806 is usually something less than impeachment where Rule 806 is not involved. Importantly, we usually do not have the person being impeached on the stand. This alone denies to us, as trial lawyers know, many wonderful opportunities – opportunities spelled out in this book.

Also, some court interpretations of Rule 806 further restrict and indeed even totally preclude our right to impeach.

A good place to start this discussion would be a review of the more important and powerful methods of impeachment and seeing how they might be effected by Rule 806.

---

[86]Rule 806: "If the party against whom a hearsay statement has been admitted calls the defendant as a witness, the party is entitled to examine the declarant from the statement as if under cross-examination."

[87]*See U.S. v. Bernal*, 719 F. 2d 1475 (9th Cir. 1983).

Inconsistent Statement Impeachment

When impeaching with an inconsistent statement you must give the witness the opportunity to deny or explain the statement. Thus, unless you actually put the declarant on the stand in your case, this would be impossible. The drafters of Rule 806 understood this problem and wisely address it in the rule. Simply stated, when using Rule 806, you need not give the declarant (who usually would not be a witness) the ". . . opportunity to deny or explain."

This language was necessary. Without it, it would have been, for the most part, impossible to impeach a Rule 806 declarant with an inconsistent statement.

Also, we are sure there was some concern with an old Supreme Court case, *Mattox v. U.S.*, 156 U.S. 237 (1895). In *Mattox* the Court would not allow the inconsistent statement impeachment where there was not, indeed could not be, an opportunity for the declarant (who was dead) to deny or explain.

Interestingly, another potential issue is left unresolved. Recall some inconsistent statement impeachment is collateral. Where it is collateral, can extrinsic evidence be used? If not, obviously there can be no impeachment.

Accepting the right to impeach with the inconsistent statement, the fact remains, absent the declarant on the stand, it will be less than totally effective. (See Chapter 1 on Inconsistent Statement Impeachment.)

Motivation Impeachment

In that the extrinsic evidence prohibition does not apply to motivation impeachments, a major issue is resolved. However, once again, the absence of the witness will have a negative effect on the impact of the impeachment. (See Chapter 2 on Motivation Impeachment.) An example can be found in a reading of *People v. Curl*, 207 P.3d 2 (Calif. S.C. 2009). The criminal defendant was denied the right to impeach a Rule 806 declarant. The intended impeachment related to motivation. Why the right to impeach was denied is difficult to understand. The facts spelled out in the opinion seem to suggest that had the defense attorney been allowed to impeach, and further, had he understood how to impeach on motivation, and, finally, had he had the witness on the stand, we may well have had a different conclusion.

Truthfulness Impeachment (Rule 608)

Here we have a major problem, one the drafters of Rule 806 probably could and should have anticipated.

Recall that Rule 608 Truthfulness Impeachment is considered collateral: extrinsic evidence is not allowed. Also recall, however, there is an exception if the seldom-used negative character evidence is used.

Absent extrinsic evidence, unless the declarant witness is called as a witness and admits to the untruthfulness, it is impossible to perfect truthfulness impeachment.[88]

In *U.S. v. Friechman*, 212 F.3d 310 (2d Cir. 1988), the court acknowledges that denying extrinsic evidence would, for the most part, render truthfulness impeachment under Rule 806 nonexistent. Acknowledging this, the Second Circuit still affirmed the conviction, even though the trial court did not allow the declarant's videotaped admission that he had lied.

U.S. v. Barrett, 8 F.3d 1296 (8th Cir. 1993) supports the use of extrinsic evidence to impeach a nontestifying declarant. At a hearing on the competency of a four-year-old, she did not know and could not explain what it meant to lie or tell the truth. The Eighth Circuit vacated the defendant's conviction, holding the denial of the defendant's right to impeach with the competency hearing denied the defendant his confrontational rights.[89]

Conversely, the Third and DC Circuits come to a different conclusion and would enforce the proscription on extrinsic evidence even when the impeachment is pursuant to Rule 806. *U.S. v. Saada*, 212 F.3d 210 (3d Cir. 2000); *U.S. v. White*, 116 F.3d 903 (D.C. Cir. 1997).

Finally we mention *U.S. v. Hall et al*, 854 F.2d 1036 (7th Cir. 1988). Though the case involves an attempt to impeach a nontestifying hearsay declarant, the defense lawyer's failure to understand impeachment renders the opinion of little or no value.

---

[88]Unless, of course, the impeachment is done through and with negative character witnesses, which is something to keep in mind in jurisdictions that do not allow extrinsic evidence when using Rule 806 impeachment.

[89]*See also U.S. v. Moody*, 903 F. 2d 321 (5th Cir. 1990) where a conviction was reversed where the defendant was denied Rule 806 impeachment intended to show the declarants had poor reputations for truthfulness.

In *Hall* there were two potential impeachment areas. One involved 609 convictions. Surprisingly, the defense did not seek to use this. The other possible potential impeachment, the one argued on appeal, apparently involved Rule 608 Truthfulness. Unfortunately, defense counsel did not understand how to do truthfulness impeachment. He simply and incorrectly asked the police officer witness whether he believed the declarant.

The drafters of the Federal Rules of Evidence did an excellent job. So also the Federal Rules of Evidence Committee continues to do an outstanding job making appropriate changes in the Rules. That said, we would strongly suggest the Committee decide the perplexing issue posed by Rule 806 where Rule 608 Truthfulness Impeachment is sought to be used. This issue would be best resolved by allowing "extrinsic" evidence. The alternative would be to admit that Rule 806 does not allow truthfulness impeachment.

Rule 609 Convictions

We have already talked about the state of the law and, more specifically, the disturbing notion that the prosecutor can, using Rule 806, impeach a nontestifying defendant with Rule 609 convictions. This issue should be revisited.

In practice, the question is how do we impeach a nontestifying defendant or witness with their 609 conviction? You can introduce into evidence a certified record of the conviction.[90] Again, some of the elegance and impact of the impeachment is lost, but the fact of the conviction comes into evidence.

Other Methods of Impeachment

All of the other methods of impeachment are, in theory, available to you. Again, the fact that the witness is usually not on the stand will substantially limit how you do your impeachment.

Also keep in mind the fact that an expert witness may testify to hearsay (Rule 703) when giving their opinion. That hearsay is subject to Rule 806 impeachment.

---

[90] *See U.S. v. Bovain*, 708 F. 2d 606 (11th Cir. 1985).

CHAPTER 13

Impeachment of a Character Witness

Actually it will unfortunately be of little concern to most prosecutors and criminal defense attorneys. Truth be known, most attorneys seldom, if indeed ever, use character witnesses. This is a mistake. That said, explaining this is not one of the purposes of this book.

In truth, most attorneys do not know how to use and present character witnesses. In particular, many criminal defense attorneys have a terrible fear of what the prosecutor will be able to do cross-examining their character witnesses.

This is somewhat ironic in that most prosecutors, who seldom have the opportunity, do not know how to cross-examine character witnesses. This is the purpose of this chapter. Actually and surprisingly, prosecutors are encouraged not to cross-examine character witnesses, as it might show bad manners.[91]

---

[91]Albeit an older prosecutor's manual reads as follows: "The Character Witness. There are specific types of witnesses who required a definite approach in cross-examination. A character witness, in particular a member of the clergy or a responded member of the community, can never by attacked as to credibility with any degree of safety. Better to leave his testimony alone than to create a feeling of hostility before the jury. Where the character

(continued)

Character evidence has been, not without reason, called a "shapeless" and "elusive" subject by no less than the United States Supreme Court. *U.S. v. Mickelson*, 335 U.S. 469 (1948). Trial manuals have, for the most part, contributed much to the confusion. That said the purpose of this chapter is not to explain the use and abuse of character evidence. Rather, as earlier mentioned, the purpose of this chapter is to explain how a character witness might properly be impeached.

To have the opportunity to cross-examine or, more specifically, impeach a character witness, the defendant must first call or put on a character witness. As mentioned, this is not done often and when done is usually not done well.

In a criminal case, Evidence Rule 404(2) allows the accused[92] to use character witnesses to prove a pertinent (translated, this means *relevant*) character trait of the accused. Sounds simple; however, many defense attorneys, having read the trial advocacy manuals or having listened to abbreviated talks on character evidence, all too often use the generic trait of "law abiding." Indeed, this was a character trait used in defending the *Mickelson* case.

The fact of the matter is the defense selection of character traits significantly limits or expands the scope of the prosecutor's cross-examination. Simply stated, if the character trait used by the defense is "honesty," the prosecutor could not impeach using an act of "violence." The prosecutor's cross-examination is limited to the character trait used by the defense. Understanding this, one can see the stupidity of using the "law-abiding" trait. Use of this trait would put few limitations on the scope of the cross-examination.

Let us then assume the defense properly and with wisdom limits the character trait. First off, the prosecutor can call *rebuttal character witnesses*.

(footnote continued from previous page)
witness is a relative of the defendant or a class friend, this can be explained, but only in a casual manner. The witness is there to prove the defendant's good character. Severe cross-examination may only prove the prosecutor's bad manners."

[92]The rule also allows, though again this is seldom used, the prosecutor to use character evidence to rebut the defense character evidence. Also, if evidence of a trait or character of the alleged victim of the crime is admitted under Rule 404(b), the same trait may be used against the defendant.

These witnesses would be limited to the defense character trait. The presentation of the witnesses would also be limited to the two ways allowed to prove character: reputation or personal opinion. Specific acts could not be used.

Accepting these limitations, prosecutors seldom, if indeed ever, use rebuttal character witnesses.

Finally, we get to the purpose of this chapter. What can the prosecutor cross-examine and impeach on?

Obviously, they can impeach using, where appropriate, our list of ways to impeach. Motive immediately comes to mind.

Significantly, prosecutors can go far beyond the traditional methods of impeachment. This is the reason for this chapter.[93]

If the character witness testified to *reputation*, the prosecutor's impeachment will start with "have you heard. . . ." Being cross-examination, we would prefer "you have heard. . .," a statement rather than a question.

If the character witness testified to a *personal opinion*, then the introductory phrase would be "do you know. . . ." Again, we would prefer "you know. . . ."

Using "heard" and "know," the prosecutor can now greatly expand the impeachment. Again, this is all subject to the "same trait" limitation, if indeed "law abiding" had not been used.

The following specific acts can be used to impeach:

1. Crimes, including those otherwise precluded by Rule 609.
2. Bad Acts
3. Arrests
4. Rumors

There are some limitations that, in truth, amount to very little.

1. The prosecutor must have a "good faith" basis for the fact used. Though, however, the prosecutor need not have a "good faith" belief that the witness does know or has heard of the fact.

[93]See an interesting law review article by Professor Richard Friedman: "Character Impeachment Evidence: Psycho-Bayesian [!?] Analysis and a Proposed Overhaul," 38 *U.C.L.A. L. Rev.* 637 (1991).

2. The prosecutor must accept the witness's answer. If the witness denies knowing or having heard of the fact, the prosecutor may not use extrinsic evidence to establish the fact. It is considered collateral.
3. The impeachment, whether the witness knew of or heard of the fact, comes in only to impeach the witness and not as substantive evidence. So what. Indeed the defense can move for a curative instruction telling the jury that what they have just heard comes in merely to impeach but not as substantive evidence. Everybody, except appellate judges, knows this is like painting racing stripes on an arthritic camel. It is, in the words of Justice Cardozo, "beyond the compass of ordinary minds."[94]
4. The prosecutor may not impeach with the crime charged in the case on trial.
5. Remoteness of the specific act may be a limiting factor. The problem for defense attorneys is that the leading Supreme Court case, *Mickelson* allowed going back thirty years (thirty and twenty-seven years, specifically) in that the character witnesses allowed that they knew the defendant that long.

---

[94]*Shepard v. United States*, 290 U.S. 96, 104 (1933) ("What the government put in evidence, however, was something very different. It did not use the declarations by Mrs. Shepard to prove her present thoughts and feelings, or even her thoughts and feelings in times past. It used the declarations as proof of an act committed by someone else, as evidence that she was dying of poison given by her husband. This fact, if fact it was, the government was free to prove, but not by hearsay declarations. It will not do to say that the jury might accept the declarations for any light that they cast upon the existence of a vital urge, and reject them to the extent that they charged the death to someone else. Discrimination so subtle is a feat *beyond the compass of ordinary minds*. The reverberating clang of those accusatory words would drown all weaker sounds. It is for ordinary minds, and not for psychoanalyst, that our rules of evidence are framed. They have their source very often in considerations of administrative convenience, of practical expediency, and not in rules of logic. When the risk of confusion is so great as to upset the balance of advantage, the evidence goes out. Thayer, Preliminary Treatise on the Law of Evidence, 266, 516; Wigmore, Evidence, ss 1421, 1422, 1714.") (emphasis added).

CHAPTER 14

Sex Offense or Sexual Assault Cases

(Four Rules of Evidence)

The US Congress, obviously responding to the electorate and following the lead of many states, decided that sexual assault and child molestation cases, be they criminal or civil, required special attention and special rules of evidence. The law as to impeachment, in these cases, would be, and accordingly is, changed.

As a result we now have Federal Rules of Evidence 412, 413, 414, and 415. These rules, for the most part, were produced by the Congress without the input or approval of the Rules Advisory Committee and the Supreme Court. This omission causes several legal issues. Again, in that this is not an evidence book, we recommend you visit an evidence book should you run into these issues. Of the many excellent evidence books, we recommend the *Federal Rules of Evidence Manual* by Saltzburg, Martin, and Capra. Professor Stephen Saltzburg is one of the very best and finest minds in the evidence field. And Professor Capra is the Reporter for the Federal Rules of Evidence.

RULE 412

Rule 412. Sex-Offense Cases: the Victim's Sexual Behavior or Predisposition.

(a) **Prohibited Uses.** The following evidence is not admissible in a civil or criminal proceeding involving alleged sexual misconduct: (1) evidence offered tto prove that a victim engaged in other sexual behavior; or (2) evidence offered to prove a victim's sexual predisposition.

(b) **Exceptions. (1) Criminal Cases.** The court may admit the following evidence in a criminal case: (**A**) evidence of specific instances of a victim's sexual behavior, if offered to prove that someone other than the defendant was the source of semen, injury, or other physical evidence; (**B**) evidence of specific instances of a victim's sexual behavior with respect to the person accused of the sexual misconduct, if offered by the defendant to prove consent or if offered by the prosecutor; and (**C**) evidence whose exclusion would violate the defendant's constitutional rights. (**2**) **Civil Cases.** In a civil case, the court may admit evidence offered to prove a victim's sexual behavior or sexual predisposition if its probative value substantially outweighs the danger of harm to any victim and of unfair prejudice to any party. The court may admit evidence of a victim's reputation only if the victim has placed it in controversy.

(c) **Procedure to Determine Admissibility. (1) Motion.** If a party intends to offer evidence under Rule 412(b), the party must: (**A**) file a motion that specifically describes the evidence and states the purpose for which it is to be offered; (**B**) do so at least 14 days before trial unless the court, for good cause, sets a different time; (**C**) serve the motion on all parties; and (**D**) notify the victim or, when appropriate, the victim's guardian or representative. (**2**) **Hearing.** Before admitting evidence under this rule, the court must conduct an in camera hearing and give the victim and parties a right to attend and be heard. Unless the court orders otherwise, the motion, related materials, and the record of the hearing must be and remain sealed.

(d) **Definition of "Victim."** In this rule, "victim" includes an alleged victim.

This rule has its origins in and was, at least initially, a "rape shield law." As such, it was intended to exclude possible impeachment based on sexual behavior or predisposition. It has been expanded to civil cases which would include claims of hostile work environment.

Criminal rape cases present problems. They are the least reported crime and, unfortunately, the complainant (others would use the term "victim," but this often puts the cart before the horse) may well be and often is subjected to not only embarrassing but also terribly abusive and questionable impeachment. On the other hand, it has long been recognized that it is easy to accuse a person of rape, though it is often difficult to prove, and even harder to defend.

Accepting these "rape shield laws," though well intended, they can and do create problems, primarily in criminal but also in civil cases.

Obviously aware of potential problems, Rule 412 attempts to anticipate and accommodate these problems. Obviously, in criminal cases a defendant has a right to defend.[95]

The sex-related rules specifically exclude impeachment offered to show the "... victim engaged in other sexual behavior." Also, the rules exclude impeachment "... offered to prove the victim's sexual predisposition."

Obviously these impeachment limitations require exceptions, and they are spelled out in Rule 412(b)(1).

Rule 412(b)(1) provides that in criminal cases the following evidence is admissible, if otherwise admissible under these rules:

(A) evidence of specific instances of sexual behavior by the alleged victim offered to prove that a person other than the accused was the source of semen, injury or other physical evidence;

(B) evidence of specific instances of sexual behavior by the alleged victim with respect to the person accused of the sexual misconduct offered by the accused to prove consent or by the prosecution; and

(C) evidence the exclusion of which would violate the constitutional rights of the defendant.

---

[95]In *Sandoval v. Acevedo*, 966 F. 2d 145 (7th Cir. 1993) the court noted that rape shield laws cannot be used to preclude a defendant from introducing vital evidence.

Civil cases also have an exception. Rule 412(b)(2) provides as follows:

> In a civil case, evidence offered to prove the sexual behavior or sexual predisposition of any alleged victim is admissible if it is otherwise admissible under these rules and its probative value substantially outweighs the danger of harm to any victim and of unfair prejudice to any party. Evidence of an alleged victim's reputation is admissible only if it has been placed in controversy by the alleged victim.

This civil exception is not a restatement of the balancing test of Rule 403. It more closely resembles the balancing test in Rule 609(b). In a word, it suggests a presumption of inadmissibility. As if that is not enough, impeachment of a civil complainant's reputation and sexual behavior is not admissible unless the complainant has placed their reputation in issue.

Though not specifically mentioned in Rule 412, the courts have wisely applied the balancing test of Rule 403 to Rule 412.

Rule 412 has a notice requirement. The party seeking to use this form of impeachment must notify their opponent and the alleged victim fourteen days before the trial, except for good cause shown, of the specific evidence sought to be used and the purpose for using this evidence.

The court then conducts a sealed-in camera hearing, which is intended not to decide the issue but rather to decide if there is an issue.

RULE 413

> **Rule 413. Similar Crimes in Sexual-Assault Cases.**
>
> (a) **Permitted Uses.** In a criminal case in which defendant is accused of a sexual assault, the court may admit evidence that the defendant committed any other sexual assault. The evidence may be considered on any matter to which it is relevant.
>
> (b) **Disclosure to the Defendant.** If the prosecutor intends to offer this evidence, the prosecutor must disclose it to the defendant, including witnesses' statements or a summary of the expected testimony. The prosecutor must do so at least 15 days before trial or at a later time that the court allows for good cause.
>
> (c) **Effect on Other Rules.** This rule does not limit the admission or consideration of evidence under any other rule.

(d) **Definition of "Sexual Assault."** In this rule and Rule 415 "sexual assault" means a crime under federal law or under state law (as "state" is defined in 18 U.S.C. § 513) involving: **(1)** any conduct prohibited by 18 U.S.C. chapter 109A; **(2)** contact, without consent, between any part of the defendant's body – or an object – and another person's genitals or anus; **(3)** contact, without consent, between the defendant's genitals or anus and any other part of another person's body; **(4)** deriving sexual pleasure or gratification from inflicting death, bodily injury, or physical pain on another person; or **(5)** an attempt or conspiracy to engage in conduct described in subparagraphs (1)–(4).

Rule 413 expands the impeachment of defendants in "sexual assault cases." Sexual assault cases are designed and spelled out in the rule.

This rule, as well as Rules 414 and 415, did not, as earlier mentioned, have the benefit of the ordinary rule-making process. For that matter, the Judicial Conference Advisory Committee on Evidence Rules, the standing Committee on Rules of Practice and Procedure, and the Judicial Conference were of the view that the rule, as well as Rules 414 and 415, constituted bad policy and should be reconsidered.

Simply explained, Rule 413 creates an exception to Rule 404 in sexual assault cases. In these cases you can now prove propensity.

The Rule 403 balancing test is not mentioned, but the courts have wisely been applying it.

Do you have to prove a sexual assault conviction to use the rule? Apparently not, a preponderance of the evidence standard will be sufficient.[96] The rule speaks about the defendant's "commission" of an uncharged offense being admissible.

The rule does have a notice requirement.

RULE 414

This is similar to Rule 413 except sexual assault cases now become "crimes in child molestation" cases.

[96] *See U.S. v. Mann*, 193 F.2d 1172 (10th Cir. 1999).

Rule 414. Similar Crimes in Child Molestation Cases.

(a) **Permitted Uses.** In a criminal case in which a defendant is accused of child molestation, the court may admit evidence that the defendant committed any other child molestation. The evidence may be considered on any matter to which is relevant.

(b) **Disclosure to the Defendant.** If the prosecutor intends to offer this evidence, the prosecutor must disclose it to the defendant, including witnesses' statements or a summary of the expected testimony. The prosecutor must do so at least 15 days before trial or at a later time that the court allows for good cause.

(c) **Effect on Other Rules.** This rule does not limit the admission or consideration of evidence under any other rule.

(d) **Definition of "Child" and "Child Molestation."** In this rule and Rule 415: (**1**) "child" means a person below the age of 14; and (**2**) "child molestation" means a crime under federal law or under state law (as "state" is defined in 18 U.S.C. § 513) involving: (**A**) any conduct prohibited by 18 U.S.C. chapter 109A and committed with a child; (**B**) any conduct prohibited by 18 U.S.C. chapter 110; (**C**) contact between any part of the defendant's body – or an object – and a child's genitals or anus; (**D**) contact between the defendant's genitals or anus and any part of a child's body; (**E**) deriving sexual pleasure or gratification from inflicting death, bodily injury, or physical pain on a child; or (**F**) an attempt or conspiracy to engage in conduct described in subparagraphs (A)–(E).

Again, the purpose of the rule is to expand impeachment. Again, contrary to Rule 404, propensity evidence will be permitted. Again, though not spelled out or mentioned, the courts have been applying the Rule 403 balancing test. Again, preponderance of the evidence is all that is required.[97]

A child is defined as someone below 14 years of age, and the offense of child molestation is spelled out in the rule.

There is a notice requirement.

---

[97]*U.S. v. Norris*, 428 F. 2d 907 (9th Cir. 2005).

RULE 415

Rule 415. Similar Acts in Civil Cases Involving Sexual Assault or Child Molestation.

(a) **Permitted Uses.** In a civil case involving a claim for relief based on a party's alleged sexual assault or child molestation, the court may admit evidence that the party committed any other sexual assault or child molestation. The evidence may be considered as provided in Rules 413 and 414.

(b) **Disclosure to the Opponent.** If a party intends to offer this evidence, the party must disclose it to the party against whom it will be offered, including witnesses' statements or a summary of the expected testimony. The party must do so at least 15 days before trial or at a later time that the court allows for good cause.

(c) **Effect on Other Rules.** This rule does not limit the admission or consideration of evidence under any other rule.

Simply stated, Rule 415 applies Rule 413 (sexual assault cases) and Rule 414 (child molestation cases) to civil cases.

Again, impeachment is expanded. Again, there is a notice requirement. Again, the impeachment may go to proving propensity. Again, though not specifically mentioned, the Rule 403 balancing test probably applies.

The rule raises potential issues in sexual assault cases.[98]

[98] *See* Aiken, "Sexual Character Evidence in Civil Action: Refining the Propensity Rule." 1997 *Wisconsin L.R.* 1221.

The Expert Witness

The senior, albeit elderly, co-author has long allowed that, if given his choice he would prefer to cross-examine an expert. Yes, even more so than the snitch who has made a "deal" and has a criminal record. This surprises most trial lawyers, many of whom do not look forward to taking on experts.

This somewhat surprising choice or preference can best be understood by learning the senior co-author has spent more than forty years trying criminal cases in the federal courts. In the federal courts, discovery to the defendant is limited. Surprisingly, not even the names of the prosecution witnesses are provided. As earlier mentioned when discussing refreshing memory (FRE 612), we were reminded the so-called Jencks Act (18 U.S.C. § 3500) protects the statements of prosecution witnesses from disclosure until *after* the witness has testified. Commendably, most federal prosecutors and judges do not insist on enforcement of this unnecessary and dumb Act.

However, where the witness is an expert, the defense attorney gets not only the name of the witness but also a summary of the testimony of the expert wtiness.[99]

With an expert witness then, we not only know who they are but we can review their *curriculum vitae*, what they have written, and earlier testimony they have given. All of this creates potential areas of impeachment.

[99]Federal Criminal Rules: Rule 16(a)(E) Documents and Objects. Upon a defendant's request, the government must permit the defendant to inspect and to copy or photograph books, papers, documents, data, photographs, tangible objects, buildings or places, or copies or portions of any of these items, if the item is within the government's possession, custody or control and: (I) the item is *material* to preparing the defense; (ii) the government intends to use the item in its case-in-chief at trial; or (iii) the item was obtained from or belongs to the defendant. Rule 16(a)(G) Expert Witnesses. At the defendant's request, the government must give to the defendant a written summary of any testimony that the government intends to use under Rule 702, 703, or 705 of the Federal Rules of Evidence during its case-in-chief at trial. If the government requests discovery under subdivision (b)(1)(C)(ii) and the defendant complies, the government must, at the defendant's request, give to the defendant a written summary of testimony that the government intends to use under Rule 702, 703, or 705 of the Federal Rules of Evidence as evidence at trial on the issue of the defendant's mental condition. The summary provided under this subparagraph must describe the witness's opinions, the bases and reasons for those opinions, and the witness's qualifications.

Most of the methods of impeachment already discussed can be potentially used on expert witnesses. In particular, we will look for inconsistent statements in their writings and earlier testimony.

Assuming the expert witness is being paid, and indeed most are, you will have motivation impeachment, not always that impactful, but motivation impeachment nonetheless. Similarly, does our expert witness always testify for the same lawyer, or at least the same side? Are they expecting, or hoping, depending on their performance, to be hired in future cases?

The "could have done but did not do" method of impeachment is usually available and effective against expert witnesses. You well may be able to use the things the expert witness could have but did not do, the information or facts that he or she does not know, particularly things they must concede would have been of interest or helpful to them.

If they spent little time in doing their work, this can be used.

Also, you may wish to suggest that they are not an expert "in doing," but rather an expert "in testifying."

Importantly, when preparing to cross-examine an expert witness we must always treat them as one would a seven hundred pound gorilla. Fortunately for the cross-examiner, the seven hundred pound gorilla is in a cage.

The last thing we want to do is get in the cage with the gorilla. To do so would be to give the gorilla all of the advantages. He knows his way around in the cage, and you are no match for him.

What we want to do is keep ourselves protected outside the cage. We have a couple (should he grab one) pool cues we will use to poke him as we walk around the cage. We also will use a slingshot to deliver a few blows and inflict some additional pain. We aggravate and attack him in a "look good," professional way, but under no circumstances do we actually wrestle with him.

Against this background we now consider two specific and independent ways to impeach experts.

CHAPTER 15
Expert's Résumé

This is not necessarily a powerful or impactful consideration when impeaching experts. Most probably for that reason, it is frequently overlooked.

Understand, we are not here talking about the expert's qualifications to be allowed to give their opinion.[100] What we here have in mind is strictly impeachment, albeit not necessarily the most powerful impeachment.

To explain. Many experts come across a bit pompous. We may be able to develop this characteristic.

Experts, not unlike many others, pad their résumés with either inaccurate information or puffing. Inaccuracies may be found in the educational degrees they list. This is surprisingly all too common. These claims can be easily verified on the Internet. Obviously this would suggest Rule 608 Truthfulness Impeachment.

---

[100]In *Daubert v. Merrell Dow Pharmaceuticals*, 509 U.S. 869 (1993), the Court changed the way federal courts interpret the admissibility of expert testimony. Its impact in replacing the former *Frye* standard was to open the gate to more evidence, with the judge acting as gatekeeper. *Daubert* focuses upon four main areas to test whether or not an expert's testimony should be admitted: (1) whether their work or idea has been peer reviewed; (2) the error rate of their methodology; (3) whether the method is accepted in their field, and to what extent; and (4) whether the method is testable and, therefore, quantifiable.

Many résumés list membership in prestigious and high-sounding organizations. Indeed, look at your own résumé and see if this is not true. Your listing such memberships should present no problems. Where, however, they are included in an expert's résumé they can be effectively, if not powerfully, used to impeach, in particular to develop his pomposity.

Q: "I want to ask you some questions about your very impressive résumé, you understand?"
A: "Yes."
Q: "For the most part, you prepared this résumé?"
A: "Yes."
Q: "You certainly wanted to list accomplishments that made you distinguished?"
A: "Yes."
Q: "And you did?"
A: "Yes."
Q: "You wanted, in particular, to list notable accomplishments?"
A: "Yes."
Q: "You wanted people who read it to be impressed with your notable accomplishments?"
A: "Yes."
Q: "Let me ask you some questions about one of the notable accomplishments you listed, you understand?"
A: "Yes."
Q: "You list your membership in the Academy of _____?"
A: "Yes."
Q: "Obviously a notable accomplishment?"
A: "Yes."
Q: "One you are proud of?"
A: "Yes."
Q: "Now I want to ask you about how you became a member of the distinguished Academy, you understand?"
A: "Yes."
Q: "You did not have to pass a test to become a member?"
A: "That's right."

Q: "You did not have to be interviewed to become a member?"
A: "Right."
Q: "You did not have to do something particularly noteworthy to become a member?"
A: "No."
Q: "But you did have to fill out and sign a one-page membership application?"
A: "Yes."
Q: "In addition to the required application you had to pay an admission fee?"
A: "Yes."
Q: "A fee of $100?"
A: "Yes."
Q: "And any _____ who completed the application and pays the $100 becomes a member?"
A: "Yes."

You also want to make a point by adversely contrasting their expert with your expert – if and where this can be done. He never took courses in the specific subject matter. He never wrote a book or articles. He is not certified (that requires more than filing an application and paying an admission fee). He has never taught at a university. He does not treat patients, and he did not treat this particular patient (he is a testing, not a treating, doctor), he does not help people get well, and he does not work with them until they are well. After he sees them (or looks at their X-rays) he does not know what happened to them. Other experts could disagree with him.

CHAPTER 16

Learned Treatises

Rule 803(18) Statements in Learned Treatises, Periodicals, or Pamphlets. A statement contained in a treatise, periodical, or pamphlet if: (**A**) the statement is called to the attention of an expert witness on cross-examination or relied on by the expert on direct examination; and (**B**) the publication is established as a reliable authority by the expert's admission or testimony, by another expert's testimony, or by judicial notice. If admitted, the statement may be read into evidence but not received as an exhibit.

This method of impeachment applies only to expert witnesses.

At common law, a cross-examiner could impeach an expert with a learned treatise. The drafters of the Federal Rules of Evidence made significant changes, more specifically they substantially expanded the common law.

- At common law, learned treatises could be used only on cross-examination. Rule 803(18) allows them to be used on direct examination as well.
- At common law, the learned treatises could be used only to impeach the expert. Rule 803(18) allows the learned treatises to come in as

substantive evidence and as an obvious exception to the hearsay rule. Just how it comes in as substantive evidence raises a few issues to be later explained.

Rule 803(18), one of the exceptions to the hearsay rule, reads as follows:

> To the extent called to the attention of an expert witness upon cross-examination or relied upon by the expert witness in direct examination, statements contained in published treatises, periodicals, or pamphlets on a subject of history, medicine, or other science or art, established as a reliable authority by the testimony or admission of the witness or by other expert testimony or by judicial notice. If admitted, the statements may be read into evidence but may not be received as exhibits.

This rule is a powerful tool or weapon when cross-examining an expert witness. Also, of course, it can be a helpful tool on the direct examination of your witness, though this is not the subject of this book. In truth, it is unfortunately seldom used on direct examination.

What qualifies as a learned treatise is spelled out in Rule 803(18). It specifically includes *published treatises, periodicals, and pamphlets.* It also includes charts and data such as a public work with widespread collegial scrutiny.

The learned treatises can be on history, medicine, science, or the arts.

The rule allows you to impeach an expert witness with something the expert did not say, and indeed something the expert may not agree with. In effect, you are impeaching the expert with an inconsistent statement opinion – except it is not his inconsistent statement or opinion. It is the statement of someone else.

We should remind ourselves of the "Fishing Rules." Where they apply and would be helpful, we will use them.

Using a learned treatise to impeach requires a basic understanding of how to do it. You must, to the satisfaction of the trial judge, establish or show that the learned treatise is "*reliable authority.*"

Though it need not be the only reliable authority, it must be a reliable authority. For the most part, the courts are liberal in finding reliable authority. For that matter, not only may the expert not agree with the reliable authority but they may not have ever read it.

You can establish or prove reliable authority in one of three ways.

The first and probably the best and easiest way to prove the learned treatise is reliable authority is through your opponents expert on cross-examination. Get him to admit he knows of the learned treatise and it is reliable authority.

As mentioned, he need not agree with the learned treatise nor even have read it, so long as he agrees it is reliable authority.

You can help him along or, if you like, set him up for the answer you want.

Q: "You have been well trained?"
A: "Yes."
Q: "You are well read in your field?"
A: "Yes."
Q: "You must stay current in your field?"
A: "Yes."
Q: "You do stay current in your field?"
A: "Yes."
Q: "You prepared yourself to be here today?"
A: "Yes."
Q: "You wanted to make sure you were knowledgeable in your field?"
A: "Yes."
Q: "You became familiar with the accepted leading works or writings in your field?"
A: "Yes."
Q: "You are familiar with _______?"
A: "Yes."
Q: "We can agree it would be a reliable authority in your field?"
A: "Yes."

Obviously, should he deny to it being a reliable authority he will come across as less than competent and honest when you use the second method to prove the work is a reliable authority.

Q: "You are telling us you never heard of _____?"
A: "Yes."
Q: "You never read it?"
A: "No."
Q: "You never saw it?"
A: "No."

Where the Expert has denied your treatise is reliable authority or simply states he never heard of your treatises, you must resort to one (most likely the second) of the other ways to establish "reliable authority."

Some years ago a brilliant criminal defense attorney, Jim Shellow, from Milwaukee, Wisconsin, had success cross-examining prosecution experts in drug cases. Jim, who has a genius IQ, would effectively use learned treatises to perfect his, as he called it, "dictionary" cross-examination.

His success apparently disturbed the DEA. Supposedly, according to Shellow, the DEA sent out to its drug experts information on how to avoid learned treatises cross-examination. They suggested they deny that treatises was authoritative. (This sure sounds like suborning perjury!)[101]

This had the effect of denying to Shellow the right to use his cross-examination to perfect his learned treatise impeachment. He could, and did establish his learned treatise but not during the cross-examination.

To be explained, there are two other ways to establish "reliable authority." The second way would require you to put a witness of your own on the stand. In the medical area you might use another doctor or the librarian at the medical school, who will be less expensive and just as effective. Let us put the librarian on the stand. Their expert is no longer on the stand to be (which is what the DEA sought to do to Shellow) impeached with the learned treatise, so you will have lost your momentum.

---

[101] *See* Cross-Examination of the analyst in drug prosecutions: James Shellow (Lexis Nexis p.99)

Sure, you can call the expert witness as an adverse witness and do the impeachment, but it will not be as effective as if you did it when you cross-examined their expert.

You would then call as a witness the librarian at the Medical School. Following the preliminaries your direct examination would go something like this.

Q: "Are you familiar with Schultz on human anatomy?"
A: "Yes, of course I am."
Q: "Why are you so familiar with this work?"
A: "It is the leading authority in the field of human anatomy."
Q: "Do the professors of your medical college use this book?"
A: "Yes, they do."
Q: "What about the students – do they make use of this book if they want to know about human anatomy?"
A: "They certainly do."
Q: "Would you consider it a reliable authority in the field of human anatomy?"
A: "It is the most used and most reliable authority in the field."
Q: "Would most doctors practicing in this area of expertise be familiar with this book?"
A: "If they were not they should not be practicing."

The third way to establish reliable authority is to get the trial judge to take judicial notice that the work is a reliable authority. Obviously we would be talking about an exceptionally well-known and accepted work.

Having established reliable authority, now things get a bit confusing. We know the learned treatise comes in as substantive evidence. However, there are limitations on how it comes in. In a word, *it may not be received in evidence* as an exhibit. In this regard it is similar to another exception to the hearsay rule, Recorded Recollection FRE 803(5). Many of us know this better as prior recollection recorded.

So what can we do with our substantive evidence? We can *read it to the jury.*

Who does the reading – you or the witness? Usually, this will or should be you unless, of course, your expert on the stand would do the better job of reading.

Finally, there is some authority allowing you to not only read the reliable authority but to show it to the jury in the form of a chart as demonstrative evidence.[102]

[102] *U.S. v. Mangan*, 575 F. 2d (2d Cir.) (Cert den. 1978).

MACCARTHY'S RULES OF TRIAL ADVOCACY

For: Leah, Donal, Jude, Deidre, Dori, Catherine, Terence and Patrick

1. The most important and necessary quality for a trial lawyer is the ability to communicate.
2. Although there have been and are many excellent evidence teachers, many of their colleagues have been a detriment to trial advocacy.
3. Always have three things. "I have said it thrice: What I tell you three times is true." Lewis Carroll: *The Hunting of the Snark*.
4. You never get a second chance to make a first impression.
5. If the jury dislikes you, it is time to fold your tent.
6. Maintaining your credibility is essential.
7. Everything you do or say during a trial is important.
8. Prepare your case backwards, starting with the jury instructions.
9. In *voir dire* it is less your picking the jury, than it is the jury picking a lawyer.
10. Body language is essential to effective communications.
11. Speak in a courtroom the way you would speak in a bar. You speak in a bar to practice speaking in a courtroom.
12. Salutations should be the exception, not the rule.
13. Trial advocacy lends itself to a variety of approaches, but make sure the one you choose works.
14. Using the rhetorical forms of speech will improve your ability to communicate.
15. Trial advocacy breakout sessions should concentrate on technique, how to do what you are doing, and not facts.
16. As the salesman or preacher your job is to persuade.
17. Your character (ethos) is critical – stress fair play and some self-deprecation.
18. Rhetorical questions, but not on cross, are most helpful; they elevate your prose and your presentation.
19. Always use an analogy in closing: see specifically R. Eugene Pincham's "sugar story."
20. The chiastic alliteration is exceptionally powerful.
21. You must "point with pride and view with alarm."
22. When the enemy is in the process of destroying itself, do not interfere.
23. Know the importance of eye contact and a smile.
24. Should you start (primacy) with weather?
25. Adjectives, as distinct from verbs, are wonderful on direct examination.
26. Do not use intensifiers – that is "very", "so", "really."
27. Do not use fillers – that is "and", "like", "ah."
28. A trial lawyer can learn much from actors, but should not be one.

29. Tell stories – at all cost avoid law school briefs.
30. Your stories should paint pictures.
31. Say to yourself "once upon a time" to get your stories started.
32. Appeal initially to emotions – a granular reaction.
33. Your jury may forget the message but will not forget you.
34. Articulate.
35. Use voice modulation.
36. Move *only* with a purpose.
37. If possible, use the "present tense."
38. Use active rather than passive verbs.
39. Primacy – start on a high note.
40. Recency – end on a high note.
41. Do not legalize. (Again see Rule 11.)
42. Use no powerless words – hedges, qualifies.
43. Carefully select the right word – and use it.
44. Find ways to identify with the jurors.
45. Milk the good.
46. Repetition (looping) helps.
47. Using a rising inflection demands an answer.
48. Never get in the cage with an expert.
49. "One fact per question" makes no sense in cross.
50. Do not "publish" an exhibit until you have finished, and then do not use the term "publish."
51. Do not agree the witness is an "expert," but merely that he can give opinions.
52. Look for "puffing" if not "mendacity" in an expert's qualifications and curriculum vita.
53. Criminal defense and plaintiffs' lawyers are not well served by "gatekeepers."
54. The "Learned Treatise" is a great tool to impeach an expert.
55. Usually the theory of the case is less important than the themes.
56. The transition is a wonderful tool to use in direct and cross-examination: it is extremely helpful on direct and essential on cross.
57. A blackboard is usually better than "PowerPoint."
58. Argument in opening statements is both wrong and of questionable value.
59. The trial judge is usually without the necessary information to rule on an "argumentative objections" during opening statement.
60. Simply mentioning a "white bear" does not paint the picture or do the job.
61. Label all persons and important things.
62. Pause at the beginning and at the end of all presentations.
63. Never move to "strike" something – it can and will not be done.
64. Cross-examination is not an "art" but rather a science.
65. If the witness is telling the story on cross-examination, you have goofed.
66. Control during cross is a good thing but not necessarily the only or even the best thing.
67. Cross that involves arguing, bickering, and quibbling is terrible.
68. Today's trial lawyers are much more skilled than their predecessors.

69. Cross and direct are the most difficult to do.
70. Wellman's *The Art of Cross-Examination* is not a good source to learn *how* to cross-examine.
71. Try as you may, you will seldom, if indeed ever, do a Perry Mason cross where the witness "confesses" on the stand.
72. On cross never let a witness "slip your punch."
73. Punish, in a mild way, the witness who denies you control during cross.
74. The "looping tool" is both proper and most helpful.
75. With few exceptions questions have no place in cross – this is not the time for the discovery channel or to find out what the case is all about. ("What was Barney Quill to you?")
76. The "no questions" exception could apply if you want to make someone "short" or "tall" or if you want something "close" or "far" away.
77. The "traditional leading question," using a tagline, need not and should not be used in cross.
78. Your story on cross should be presented with short statements.
79. On cross get the witness into the "yes" mode and you can do wonderful things.
80. Many witnesses will say something that is wrong, stupid, or deceptive, something the jury will recognize as such. You use "plausibility" cross to "milk" this.
81. Your source material on cross, in addition to what the witness said on direct and possible impeachment, will consist of the witness statements, verisimilitude, and plausibility.
82. On cross, dominate the witness, but do so without appearing domineering.
83. If you screw up, leave and go to a safe haven.
84. Impeachment is not limited to matters of credibility.
85. Trial lawyers and judges know less about impeachment than any other aspect of the trial.
86. There are at least sixteen and not merely five ways to impeach a witness.
87. Impeachment with inconsistent statements is the most used and most important method of impeachment.
88. Most trial lawyers know little about how to impeach with an inconsistent statement.
89. There are times, when it is not collateral, when you should *not* "recommit" an impeaching statement.
90. You must extol the original impeaching statement.
91. You must close possible escape hatches when impeaching with an inconsistent statement.
92. Notwithstanding the Federal Rules of Evidence, show the witness the impeachment statement.
93. Anytime the Federal Rules of Evidence say you no longer have to do it the old way, continue to do it the old way.
94. Who reads the inconsistent statement – you or the witness?
95. Do both – have the witness read the statement and you also read (use the "looping tool") the statement.
96. Inconsistent statement may or may not be collateral.
97. Motivation impeachment is never collateral.
98. Truthfulness impeachment is always collateral.
99. When something good happens on direct or more particularly on cross, "*milk it.*"
100. Avoid adjectives on cross – that is "*large* clock."

101. Ethics is not only important but exceptionally difficult.
102. Lord Carson's cross-examination of Oscar Wilde was not very good.
103. Use motions in liminie.
104. Defending a criminal case always submit "theory of the case" instructions.
105. Defending a criminal case always consider the use of character testimony.
106. If selecting a "pertinent" character trait, *never* use "law abiding."
107. If a defendant testifies the "truthfulness," character trait has little downside.
108. The other side's witnesses "tell their version" or their "story": your witnesses "testify."
109. It is usually easier to get forgiveness than permission.
110. The commandment to not ask the "one question too many" makes no sense.
111. The commandment to not "repeat the direct" often makes sense – but not always: what if the witness says something good on direct?
112. On cross-examination it is better (with one exception when "tweaking") not to call the witness by name or make mention of a witness's "honorific."
113. In opening statement you do not suggest what the evidence will show: rather you say you will prove whatever it is.
114. When faced with an evidence objection, look at the judge and with your head nodding up and down, start with "as your Honor well knows," hopefully followed by a legal citation.
115. Do not assume a burden you do not have.
116. When faced with "facts beyond change," do not fight them.
117. Be yourself, as Oscar Wilde observed, "everybody else is taken."
118. You do the "bragging" for your expert witness.
119. If the defendant will testify, you tell his story in the opening statement.
120. Avoid the stupid direct examination questions: "state your full name for the record and spell your last name for the court reporter"; "directing attention . . . what, if anything, unusual occurred?"; "did there come a time . . .?"
121. Primacy helps direct: "why are you here testifying?"
122. When you get something good in cross or direct "loop it" by repeating it (three times) and writing it on the blackboard.
123. Maintaining control during cross-examination is important, but if the witness looks bad in denying your control, you will gain more than maintaining control.
124. Do not walk and talk at the same time.
125. Anger and arrogance are desirable in their witness but not in yours.
126. A theory of the case is important and usually easy to figure out: your story line will come from the themes in your case, both good and bad.
127. Get rid of the salutations in opening statement – start with primacy.
128. Never waive an opening statement.
129. The lectern is for putting things on not for standing behind.
130. Do not hold a writing instrument (unless you are using it on a blackboard) in your hand while talking.
131. In a criminal case the prosecutor has to convince twelve jurors. The defense need only "confuse" one.
132. Three things can happen after a criminal jury trial. Two of them favor the defendant.
133. When you find yourself in a deep hole, quit digging.

INDEX

9 781634 254205

Printed by Libri Plureos GmbH in Hamburg,
Germany